WITH LOVE FROM
BRATISLAVA

CHRISTY MORGAN

ISBN 978 1 717 70104 6

Imprint: Independently published

https://goo.gl/4DAFSJ

Cover Design by Scarlett Rugers Design www.scarlettrugers.com
Cover Image *Michalská brána a hrad* by Lucia Chocholackova www.luccho.com

With heartfelt thanks to R, J, S, K, L, M, T, D, and G –
and to any other letters that I may have inadvertently missed.

The object of life is not to be on the side of the majority,
but to escape finding oneself in the ranks of the insane.
— Marcus Aurelius

CHAPTER ONE

Sometimes, fleeting moments of banal ordinariness can spark something of a revolution. For me, it began with a "Hiya!"

It had been three years since I had last heard from Józef. Life, as it is wont to do, had distracted us from each other's thoughts, with only the occasional post on social media dancing on the periphery of our mutual awareness. I had moved to Canada, married Andy, and had three miscarriages followed by two little boys since we'd parted acrimoniously outside my apartment in Kiev ten years before.

Józef finally donned a golden band on his own ring finger, which no doubt had come as quite the shock to the dozen or so women who had attempted to manoeuvre him into that status before her. From what I understood, his wife was someone he barely knew at the time of their marriage; a university student who had spent more time admiring him during his lectures than having much opportunity to comprehend the inner workings of his complex soul. But it has to be said that the timeline and depth of love upon marriage is sometimes neither here nor there, though an unplanned pregnancy can certainly help to speed things along rather nicely. So, they married, and pleased both families, and settled down to a life of unexpected domesticity, at least on his part.

Józef was already familiar with being a father thanks to his teenage son from a youthful relationship that had gone the way that youthful relationships often do. Far from regretting how early in life parenthood had been thrust upon him, Józef adored the boy and was enormously proud of every milestone and achievement. Romantic relationships may have been a perpetual puzzle to him, but from my observations, he was a natural at being a dad.

When I eventually heard of his marriage, I judged it best to keep my distance. Anyway, Józef was a terrible correspondent, even at the best of times. It was unlikely he had even noticed my quiet withdrawal.

In this way, time and distance and my new life did away with any nostalgic longings of my heart, and our occasional attempts to keep in touch no longer pained me as they might have once done.

In spite of his intolerance for political correctness, his disinclination for radical feminism and mass immigration, the speed with which he complained about restaurant meals if something wasn't served to his rather exacting standards, and his seemingly–unconquerable fecklessness with money, Andy, on the other hand, was a very decent husband and an exceptionally good parent.

Despite the oft–repeated stories of his youthful antics and rock band singing that had initially fed my attraction to him, with their luscious hints of adventure and authority–bucking, as a boyfriend and then as a husband in his more serious years, this edge had mellowed into absolute contentment for the non–eventful ordinary. He was, by his own admission, grateful to be living an uncomplicated existence made easier still by my cooking and cleaning and organisation of both of our lives. My very gradual disappointment in the illusion of his ambitiousness, his deep unwillingness to make decisions unless pushed; these gnawed at my heart and chipped away at my acquiescence until they edged me ever closer to the brink of ferment. But at the time, he was the perfect antidote to Józef, with his refreshing straightforwardness and refusal to play games with women.

This was not to say that he was the major cause of my existential discontent. It was not his fault, and I refused to aim the dart of blame at him in my heart. He had never made a secret of his character or goals; it was I who had misinterpreted what was clearly in front of me.

Feeling trapped by the tethers of domesticity, disillusioned by the sluggish monotony of country living, and utterly disconnected from my old friends and former life, I was petrified that this was, in fact, *it*. This was the rest of my life. The dreams and ambitions and desires I had formerly been so passionate about, it was all beginning to slip away in the interminable shackles of duty and societal expectations, pinned down by the honourable bounds of till death do us part.

Had it not been for the catalyst of that *hiya*, it is likely that my despondency for the direction my life was cantering towards would have remained just that.

CHAPTER TWO

On a Sunday evening in late September, with the windows thrown open to let in the pine–scented gloriousness of the country breeze, I was working on a client project in my home office. Nothing out of the ordinary. The children were finally asleep, and Andy was outside having a joint on the back deck under a magnificent tablecloth of stars. Our three cats fisticuffed in and out of the room in search of scratches and treats, while the radiator made an occasional tick in the boys' bedroom as it came to life again after a long summer of unemployment. The occasional hoot of an owl or wincing screech as a fox pounced on its prey were all that broke the utter stillness of rural Prince Edward Island heading into its nocturnal slumber.

Bing.

A message notification flashed in the bottom–right of my lap–top screen. I glanced at it casually, wondering who could be messaging me at that hour.

Józef.

I froze.

A tiny thrill at his name competed with an instinctive tug of unwillingness to engage in any exchange that would inevitably dissipate into another year or three of silence between us.

I kept on working. Just ignore it for now.

Blink.

Unclicked, the notification flashed for my attention.

Look, I chided myself, there was no rush to reply. It had been one, two years since the last message. As long as I didn't click on the notification, it would officially remain unread, and there was no immediate expectation of a reply. Ignore.

Blink. Blink.

Somehow, I found myself clutching the mouse, its cursor hovering just so over the notification. There it flickered in response, waiting for me to just click.

Blink. Blink.

Blink.

That *hiya*, I supposed, should not be ignored. A *hiya* must also, in general, be responded to. It wasn't asking too much of me to be polite, surely. Cursory courtesies. That's all.

I stared at my lap–top screen, pondering the most appropriate response to such a minefield of a greeting.

I weighed, and I considered, before opting for a safely unoriginal *hiya* in return.

There. I'd done it.

Józef replied immediately, enquiring how I was.

"Good, thanks, you?"

"Good."

"How is your family?"

"Good. Yours?"

"Good."

Several moments ticked by with no further elaboration to this stimulating repartee. I began to relax. Then:

"Actually. There is something of a crisis with my son's mother."

At least he got straight to the point.

"Oh my god – is she OK?"

"Yes, she's well. She moved out two weeks ago."

"I'm so sorry. Are you OK?"

"Yes. It seems the grass is greener on the other side. How are you?"

"I think we've established that I'm well."

"Good. I'm happy to hear from you. Actually, I was just thinking about the good old days in Dublin."

The good old days in Dublin. I smirked. What an imagination. I wasn't sure *I* could look back on our time there in quite the same way.

To paint a backdrop to this reminiscence, we had lived together for several months in a white Lilliputian apartment at the top of an old Georgian building on Lower Leeson Street in Dublin, in what had once been the nursery quarters. We'd met at a training course in Belgium just over a year before, the topic of which I'd long forgotten, but the impression of his sensuous sense of authority I would never forget. There was something about it that I had found so thrilling, thanks to my highly–romantic view of the world in my late twenties. We'd got together after I took a long weekend trip to his country two weeks later on the back of a few emboldening glasses of wine and the remembrance of his Slavic attractiveness. Somehow, our relationship advanced through my monthly visits and a single trip to Dublin by Józef, whose side teaching responsibilities kept him to a tight lecture schedule during the academic year. I was carried away by the perceived romance of it all: the mysterious boyfriend, the foreign trips, the pastoral beauty of the Polish countryside, and his family's cottage in an old–fashioned village. These impressions daubed the cracks in our relationship for longer than they ought, with one of us too worldly about women, the other thoroughly naïve about men.

At the time, I had been in Dublin for more than seven years, and could honestly see myself never living anywhere else but there – or, perhaps, a certain country in Eastern Europe – for the rest of my life.

Józef, dissatisfied with nameless issues that he would not share, had eventually persuaded us both that him moving to Ireland would be the cure–all for everything wrong with his life. I'd been feeling gradually uneasy by his slow emotional and physical withdrawal – not that he was the physically–affectionate type anyway – but I couldn't put my finger on exactly what was going on. Yet Józef seemed in no hurry to end our relationship. So, I continued to excuse away the niggles of head over heart, and blindly trusted that things would work themselves out in time.

Now, thrilled at the possibility of finally converting our long–distance relationship into something more stable – despite those insistent pokes of misgiving – I tapped into my connections to help Józef land a job that both increased his seniority and his income.

He moved to Ireland, working late each night at his consulting projects before disappearing every weekend back home. He was always gone from Friday afternoon until the Monday morning, insisting that he needed to spend time with his young son. I forced myself to ignore any clues that hinted at other commitments.

I felt it would be selfish to ask him to give the weekend trips up, or even spend one weekend a month with me in Ireland. He somehow never thought to invite me to his country, nor did I feel I had the right to suggest it, seeing as we now lived together. I got along very well with his adorable mother, and regretted not being able to see her as much as I had in the past. But what could I do? I was too afraid of what rocking the boat might bring.

This awkward arrangement puttered on for five more depressing months. That is, until an acquaintance of mine who ran a local hotel slid a booking confirmation for a two–guest room in Józef's name through the front door of my building. The booking was for the very same night he was headed to Cork in the south for business. 'Private' was underlined twice on the envelope beside my name, leaving a slight puncture under the last three letters to hint at the pen's urgency.

I had frozen, numb with the horror of absolute disbelief, as I stared at that piece of paper.

Rationally, I *knew* exactly what the room booking meant, but my heart desperately churned out every shred of rationalisation it could come up with.

Coincidentally, not twenty minutes beforehand I'd poked my head out of our living room window as Józef headed to the intercity coach at the top of the street, hoping to catch his eye and wave a cheery goodbye before he left for Cork. I'd idly wondered why he'd turned around and walked back towards the corner of Leeson and Hatch, before stopping suddenly to think. Perhaps he'd forgotten something at home, I'd wondered. My phone had rung at that very moment, so I'd run to answer it in case it was him. By the time I stuck my head out the window again, less than a minute later, Józef and the coach were gone.

Now that envelope, combined with the map I'd seem him scrutinise on our bed the day before, his unprompted mention of having gone twice to confession recently, and his declaration that he didn't want to be the reason for me learning Polish, had still left me utterly unprepared for the devastation that immediately followed that black–and–white confirmation of his presumed infidelity.

When I finally got a hold of him, Józef would neither confirm nor deny what the room booking strongly implied. Instead, like a deer trapped by a lion, he saw this opportunity as a gap in the woods and made a dash for freedom with no explanation.

In the wake of the separation that inevitably followed, I made desperate plans to leave Ireland. It was the only response I could think of to escape this agony. I wasn't sure where or how, only why. My beloved Ireland could be mine no more with him still living there, breathing its air. Józef had tainted the romance of Dublin for me, perhaps forever. I would not, could not, stay.

As the quickest route to getting out of there, I decided to transfer to the first international office of the company I was working for that had a semi–suitable vacancy. I almost didn't care where, so long as it wasn't there. I was grateful for the support of my practical and empathetic manager, who threw all his weight into supporting me.

The head of the Ukrainian office took one look at my résumé and immediately negotiated with my manager for an interview. The fact that Ukraine and Józef's country were so close to each other, I forced myself to absolutely dismiss from my mind. This time, I was determined to think purely with my head. The opportunity to take on a senior management role in a thoroughly different culture would be, I hoped, the best distraction for my personal misery, and the most strategic step for any career progression I might obtain.

So, I jumped on a plane, did well enough at the interview, and within four weeks moved to Kiev in the depths of a tempestuous winter.

I was right; Kiev *was* an incredible distraction. Before long, the daily curiosity of living in this extraordinary city soon quelled any depression I'd brought along with me, and my spirits began to sing again as I immersed myself in all the diversions that Kiev had to offer. Strangely enough, one of my greatest pleasures was the local MegaMarket supermarket, with its (to me) exotic food and Cyrillic hieroglyphics glossing the necessary ordinary in thrills of mystery.

Just as I had begun to put the past behind me, Józef reappeared in my life a few months later, just as the dust on my Ukrainian move had settled and I was slowly moving on with my life.

His stated reason for suggesting a visit was a long–standing curiosity about Ukraine, which was to jointly host the World Cup with Poland in the not–too–distant future. He simply wanted to come and see what it was like. As the time of his proposed visit drew closer, however, this was converted to an invitation for me to travel to his country, as his workload would not enable him to take a break after all. It also meant that I could see his mother again, who had kept in occasional touch all this time.

I accepted the change of plans with misgivings, and sorely regretted not listening to myself when he wounded my heart yet again with the inevitable break of unspoken promises while I was there.

Yes, I know, I know.

I swore, absolutely never again.

Yet, three months later, Józef was there in Kiev itself. He'd come with one of his best friends who, in the end, decided to pursue other temptations rather than the planned boys' weekend. Józef was left to find his own entertainment and, unless he wanted to share the hotel room with his friend and his new 'friends', Józef had to find somewhere else to stay.

And, well, I had more to regret that to pride myself on from the two nights that followed.

Then, once again, he was out of my life. Yet another move was before me: two weeks later I took an English teaching job in Germany. I no longer gave a damn about corporate politics or pleasing faceless shareholders or discussing the latest sales figures. Instead, I would teach business English to engineers at Siemens in Karlsruhe, which was very close to the French border.

I naturally hoped that this was finally it with him. There was something to be said for thoroughly despising my own ridiculousness.

Four months later, Józef's call, text, then email one evening in early February remained unanswered for several hours.

I had met Andy on the first day of my new job in Karlsruhe. We soon discovered an affinity in having run away from unhappy relationships and unsatisfactory jobs. We were further drawn together by a refreshing combination of good humour and openness. Within three months, we were living together with three cats and a balcony of herbs and vegetables, luxuriating in the uncomplicated nature of an oh–so–straightforward relationship. It was all that I needed at that time, and I was tremendously grateful to Andy for giving it to me.

Józef's messages had gone unnoticed that night by the sounds of the radio and frying pan clashing for attention as Andy and I made dinner together and joked around. I eventually messaged Józef back – somewhat gleefully, it must be said – to announce my new relationship. He quietly disappeared, and all communications between us came to an end for quite some time.

From then on, I only heard from him every couple of years. Enough water had now passed under the bridge that the remembrance of past disappointments had been softened by my more transparent relationship with Andy, and sugar–coated into innocuousness by the knowledge that I was unlikely to ever see Józef again.

So, with this convoluted history as my reference, I knew well enough not to get caught up with any rose–tinted glassing now that Józef and I were both married to others, no matter how many years had whizzed by us in the interim. Nine years were a long time. Perhaps we could finally engage in a friendship free of games and confusion.

To my surprise, Józef kept in regular touch over the next few weeks, always assured of friendly – if cautious – support from me as he navigated the early days of his separation and the reestablishment of his single identity.

However, there was an unexpected side–effect to him getting in touch with me again after all these years. I was becoming increasingly aware of how this continual re–connection to someone linked so closely to my younger self was feeding that growing knot of dread about my present life. I kept interrogating myself, was I really willing to continue suppressing the regret of living in discontent, for the sake of everyone and everything except myself?

If the horse you're riding falls over, you get off. Right?

Soon enough, I knew that I had to get off.

CHAPTER THREE

It was an eventuality that I anguished over for three desperate days, alternately determined to push on with my decision to tell Andy that this must somehow come to an end, before my courage quivered against the intoxicating familiarity of the status quo. Whichever option I chose, it would bring with it the end of an ideal and a reality. There was no right or wrong; only a decision that had to somehow be made.

Me, the usually effortless decision–maker – I grappled with the knowledge that this was being driven by me and me alone. And it wasn't as if I had a firm plan in mind. I just knew that I had to get myself away, to get back to Europe where I most belonged, and to figure out the next steps in my life from there. Once the decision was made, surely a plan would follow.

On the eve of the third day, once the children were tucked up in bed and I was made bold by a half–bottle of red wine and Andy mellowed by some pot, I shared my decision with him. It took quite a few minutes to clearly get it all out, with the fear and sorrow behind what I had to say constricting my throat as I pushed myself to recite the words I'd memorised and then half–forgotten in the figurative punch of that awful moment.

Despite my intimate knowledge of Andy and his ways, I literally had no idea how he would react outside my various imaginings of this scene. Although fairly easy–going for the most part, he did have a temper when he felt himself cornered. I was more or less alone in his country, after all, with his well–to–do father just a phone call away. If I didn't play my cards right, I had a fantasy of horror that the lawyer in his large Macedonian–Canadian family in Toronto – a multimillionaire second–cousin with bulldog sway and extensive influence –

would be called in to protect his relative's interests. A far–fetched fear, perhaps, but not entirely improbable.

To my considerable relief, Andy's actual response was one of quiet tears as he slowly comprehended what I was telling him. There was no surprise, no acrimony, just acceptance.

In all honesty, Andy had known deep down in the recesses of his subconsciousness that I wasn't fulfilled. He was well–aware of the dreams I had put on hold, the plans I had quashed over the years while we struggled to get our various business ventures off the ground in the hope of a better life. The English language vacation company we'd founded when we'd moved to Canada had lasted for a good couple of years, but rural Nova Scotia where we first settled was just too out–of–the–way for international students, no matter how beautiful the location. Once the children had come along, we closed down the business and moved to Charlottetown on Prince Edward Island to give Tom and Pat more opportunities. It was certainly livelier, but still, it was really no more than a big town that hummed merrily along at its own sweet unhurried pace.

Existential and marital frustrations began to affect me more so than Andy, as throughout our relationship I had dealt with domestic responsibilities and miscarriages and pregnancies as well as my own work, all while championing and pushing him. Andy had often promised that we'd eventually move back to the rich bustle of Europe. But the money and opportunity were just never there, and soon enough his interest in the whole idea flitted away into nonchalance. Then the babies began turning into active little boys, and any discussions about the future beyond the immediate were stalemated for yet another day that never seemed to arrive.

Andy had been conscious of all this, but yet had secretly hoped that somehow it would all just go away. Truthfully, there had genuinely been a time when he too wanted to move back while our life abroad was still fresh in his mind. But the routine realities of daily existence had at some point eclipsed his more tenuous nostalgia. If Andy was honest with himself – and he was usually bluntly honest with himself – then he would have to admit that he simply didn't have an interest in the alternative. He had always been more practical than sentimental, a trait underscored by parenthood. His life was now firmly rooted on Prince Edward Island, where his IT skills were a valuable commodity in this smaller community. In his opinion, it would be foolish to give it all up before he'd given it the best shot he could.

Now though, the day of reckoning had finally arrived. Although Andy was fully aware that his own recalcitrance had pushed him into the corner he now found himself in, it still came as a sharp shock that I was really going to leave him.

I remember how we stared at each other for a very long moment as my words sank in, before both of us looked away, lost in our separate thoughts.

To give Andy the credit he deserved, it was a testament to his decency and respect that if I had come to this decision, and was determined to act upon it, then he believed without any doubt that I had thought it out and felt it the absolute right thing to do for the both of us. At age four and five, the children were remarkably well–adjusted and outgoing, and well–used to an ever–changing environment full of interesting people. Since Tom's earliest days being breastfed between classes when we ran our business in Nova Scotia, to the comings and goings of donors, volunteers, and people in need through the food charity I ran on the island, both children were very open and curious little boys. They would be fine with whatever path we planned out.

And so, Andy did not resist. He just let me go.

Over the next few awkward days, we began adjusting to this new reality. We were both in agreement that the boys should not know that we had separated – not now, not yet. Instead, we'd tell them that I had some work to do in Europe and that Andy had to stay in Canada to look after his business, but that he would visit us often and would of course bring plenty of maple syrup. After showing them pictures on the internet of indoor playgrounds and food and Christmas markets and all the other fun things they'd get to do, the boys took to the news with great excitement.

Andy left me to my own thoughts for the most part, while I tried to figure out the actualities of where to go and what to do. I sought his advice on this idea or that as they occurred to me, and he offered his opinions or suggestions willingly. In the meantime, we continued living together, even sleeping in the same bed and carrying on much as we usually did in all other respects.

By great good chance, I found us an excellent lawyer through the provincial referral service, where legal practices offered an initial consultation for next to nothing in the hopes of gaining clients who might otherwise go elsewhere.
On a sharply chilly morning in late autumn, we drove to the lawyer's office to chat with him about our options. We brought with us our draft separation

agreement, which I'd written myself and cleared with Andy. I was determined to be both thorough and fair, and to do away with as much stress as I possibly could for Andy. This hadn't been his choice, after all, and his support was necessary to fulfil my dreams. The terms of the draft agreement nodded to both my generosity and my guilt: Andy would keep the furniture, as well as the tools and other contents of the shed; he would also receive 60% of the nett proceeds from selling the house. He would keep the funds from selling our car, in return for taking care of my beloved pet cat for the duration of its life unless I was in a position to eventually take him abroad with me.

Our lawyer, an older, pragmatic gentleman with a strong interest in history and an office bursting with souvenirs from his foreign travels, was fascinated by our story.

"I don't see many cases at all where the partners are in such harmony about their decision so early in the process," he marvelled. "And I certainly don't remember the last time a couple came to me with a fourteen–page separation agreement, especially one that both parties have agreed to in theory."

Andy and I looked at each other and smiled.

"Well, this certainly makes my job a lot easier if you decide to go ahead with my services," he continued.

It was speedily agreed that yes, he was the right fit for us, and that we would appreciate his guidance about international custody agreements as well as the separation agreement. Andy and I were mutually adamant about both of us having equal custody rights to begin with, with no legal restrictions on Andy's ability to visit the children whenever he chose. In return, he promised to never keep the children in Canada without my notarised consent. No financial provisions for child support were set, which the lawyer shook his grey head at and urged us to reconsider.

On my side, I knew from the experiences of numerous friends the bitterness that can creep in to negotiations when one party who cannot afford to provide support, is pressed by the law to do so, even if they are morally and rightly obliged to. I didn't want to see things go that way with Andy, especially when I needed his backing so badly.

On Andy's side, he wanted to be a man about his responsibilities, to strive to work harder from this moment on to honour his financial commitments. Noble – and perhaps naïve – in objective reasoning our financial agreement might be, Andy and I felt the arrangement reflected both our wishes and our mutual motivation to push very hard to make this a success.

Clear in our decision and with no legal objections to offer aside from the child support counsel, the lawyer handed my draft separation agreement to his assistant to prepare in proper legal form. At the same meeting, it was also agreed that he would handle the legalities of selling our house once it was put on the market.

With that, he shook hands with us, and promised to call as soon as the document was ready to be signed.

CHAPTER FOUR

I now began to turn my thoughts more fully to how I would support myself abroad.

Whatever I made from my share of the house would go towards the move and somewhere to live. Andy would of course go halves with the plane tickets and school fees, but he drew the line at helping with groceries or utility bills. It was my decision to leave and, after all, he had his own bills to pay. He would, however, take on the burden of any shared debts until I had a regular enough income to contribute to these.

As much as I disliked the idea of teaching English full–time, I had to admit it was probably the most achievable route to getting a visa to wherever I ended up going. So, I kept a close eye on teaching jobs published online over the next few days, applying for the most interesting opportunities as they caught my fancy. I also sent my updated résumé off to a few contacts, who promised to get in touch if anything came up. One thing I was absolutely sure of: if I was going to throw myself out there again on this uncertain little adventure, I wanted to go somewhere that felt familiar, yet a little bit different to what I'd experienced before. Ireland was therefore ruled out, as comforting as it would have been to slip back into my old life and long–standing friendships. Germany, as much as I loved the way of life and spoke some of the language, was also excluded. On my handwritten list, scribbled in no particular order, were Switzerland, Austria, Slovakia, Slovenia, Liechtenstein, Andorra, Luxembourg, Croatia, and Bulgaria. Greece, France, and Italy had question marks against them on account of what I'd heard about red tape. The UK was a no for similar reasons to Ireland.

Scrolling through the job listings one morning before Andy and the kids were up, coffee in hand, with my cat Jack kneading his claws into my lap in blissful ignorance, my eye was immediately caught by a colourful advertisement.

> *Our international school is looking for an English teacher. We are a private kindergarten and elementary school in Nitra, Slovakia with a special licensed program focused on learning languages. We are looking for an open–minded, active, and creative professional to join our young staff of foreign teachers. In our facilities, kids learn subjects such as art, geography, science, and mathematics through the English, Spanish and/ or Chinese language. We also have different sport programs taught by specialists as well as a wide variety of special weekly activities that include international cooking, field trips, special dates celebrations, and more.*

I quickly looked up on the map exactly where Nitra was. It was about an hour to the north–east of Slovakia's capital, Bratislava, and within easy reach of the Austrian border.

The post further elaborated that the role was to fill a maternity leave vacancy, and would be available from April for at least one year. So far, so good. I checked out their website, and was instantly wowed by the facilities and the great lengths they'd gone to in order to make it as visually attractive as possible to little ones. It didn't take long to convince myself that this sort of school would be absolutely perfect for the boys, and would go a long way to furthering their excitement about the move.

Soon enough, I heard Andy fumbling in the kitchen making his first cup of coffee of the day. I enthusiastically called him into the room to show him the ad and the school website.

Despite his half–awake state, Andy was equally impressed by the information. Without hesitation, he encouraged me to apply immediately. He'd lived in Slovakia for several years before moving to Germany, and had very fond memories of the culture and its people. If I was going to move away with the children, then he strongly preferred that they go somewhere he was already familiar with if that option presented itself.

I speedily typed up a cover message, attached my résumé, and hit the send button. To my delight, within twenty–four hours I received a request to do a video interview with the school's HR Manager, scheduled for the very next day.

The interview with the bubbly recruiter went very well ("You're perfect! I'm very happy with this meeting", she declared). The follow–up interview with the school's director was equally positive, if much more cool and noncommittal at this early stage. However, with the average teaching applicant being a recent graduate with almost no experience whatsoever, and with the majority preferring bigger cities in more familiar European countries, it wasn't too much of a leap to imagine why they were interested in me. Not only that, but I brought with me the necessary qualifications complemented by a practical comprehension of child psychology, and would be enrolling my two fee–paying children to sweeten the deal.

The director informed me at the end of the conversation that she would speak to the HR Manager, and arrange for the necessary paperwork to be drawn up if I'd like to go ahead.

Deep down, as I soon began to admit to myself, I wasn't so absolutely excited about the idea of spending eight hours a day or more with a group of small children that were not my own. But I was a good teacher and I genuinely loved kids, so I knew I could do it if I really put my heart into it. Besides, the opportunity was almost too perfect in every respect.

Requests for interviews with other schools across Europe began to follow as my résumé made its way out there, but if I was going to do this, my heart was set on the international school in Slovakia for the sakes of Pat and Tom.

Although Andy felt that Bratislava would be a better location given its larger size and access to more cultural opportunities, Nitra was after all just a stone's throw away. Perhaps it was better to start small while we got used to our new life, and then move to Bratislava once the teaching contract was up.

In the meantime, Andy was still in full agreement that the school seemed incredible in look and in curriculum. As experienced English teachers, we were both equally passionate about meaningful, interesting education.

Józef, too, was encouraging, and calculated the distance by car should I accept his offer to come and help us get settled in those first few days.

Although my discussions with the school were going reasonably well, I continued to have those niggling doubts about how fulfilled I would be teaching small children. The more I thought about it, the more convinced I became that this wasn't truly for me.

I wondered, however, if it was somehow possible to move to Nitra and do something else, while still sending the kids to that amazing school. Couldn't

I surely continue doing what I was doing as a freelance professional? I enjoyed supporting people with their résumés and cover letters and interview coaching and all the other services that I provided as a consultant to job seekers. My clients came from all around the world, and the work was done by email and telephone, anyway. The majority of my clients were non–native speakers looking for work in English–language environments. Wouldn't Europe be the perfect location to continue doing this?

It was Andy who came up with the idea for me to start my own consulting business there. By this time, I was reasonably convinced that Slovakia would be the best place to begin my new adventure. I confess that I knew very little about the country at that time, aside from what Andy had told me, but it really did sound ideal.

"I had a sole trader license when I lived there. You can get a temporary residency permit off the back of that, and just work for yourself. You can apply as soon as you get there. You'd just have to look up how much you need these days to prove you have enough savings. Back then, it was the equivalent of three or four thousand euro, tops. But if you're going to do it, go to Bratislava though. Don't go to Nitra. Nitra's nice and all that, but I lived there for a few months before I moved to Bratislava, so I know about both. Bratislava has more cultural stuff and networking opportunities, and probably more international schools, too."

I was intrigued by the idea of just being self–employed. But the ease of getting temporary residency through a sole trader license seemed too good to be true, quite frankly. So, we quickly jumped online and did some research. Sure enough, it was still one of the most popular routes for foreigners going to Slovakia to work. The fact that the country wasn't the most obvious choice for the typical economic migrant in Europe made it that much more attractive to me.

I was sold. It had been quite a few years since I'd worked for anyone but myself, so the thought of doing a nine–to–five job had filled me with not a little trepidation. I couldn't care less about targets and doing what I was told to do by someone else. My decade of working for a global company earlier in my career had thoroughly turned me off massive corporations and the relentless pursuit of revenue and penny–pinching for the ultimate benefit of unknown shareholders who didn't give a damn about the people, only that they received their dividends. Performance reviews, team meetings, sales forecasts, budget cuts, redundancies – ugh. It had, however, left me with a genuine interest in the employee and job seeker side of the equation: the individuals who were unwitting chess pieces in this universal revenue game. I'd by this point built up a strong enough reputation in the consulting world, that it would be a shame to give it all up for the unknown.

Coincidentally, around this time Andy received two separate phone calls almost back–to–back from big tech companies. Both were in need of a field service partner on Prince Edward Island to do installations and service calls on behalf of their national clients. The existing tech for one of the companies was retiring and hadn't been able to handle the ever–increasing workload; the other company was just expanding into the province and didn't have anyone on the ground yet. The timing was incredible. This couldn't have come at a better time for his pocket or as a distraction. If all went well, these contracts would be worth hundreds of thousands of dollars per year. And they needed him to begin work almost immediately.

Andy could finally afford to hire a junior technician to support him. Within a week, he'd found an enthusiastic young tech who was thrilled at no longer having to work for one of the many low–paying companies he'd worked for in the past. Andy was now set.

CHAPTER FIVE

With my own rough plan in place and Andy urgently needing to move closer to town for his work, now was the right time to put our house on the market.

We had owned Darlington Gables for less than a year, a gift from Andy's father. Of course, I naturally felt a decent level of guilt at the proceeds now being used to fund our separate lives, but I knew it was an investment in his grandsons' future that would ultimately be worth far more than seemed justified right now. Anyway, Andy's intention was to buy a smaller house in town and use it as both a home and office, so a good portion of the money would be swiftly re-invested back into property.

The very same high-spirited realtor who'd overseen the house purchase only ten months before, was naturally quite surprised at representing us again so quickly as sellers. Ava Chaisson had a fantastic reputation for selling properties swiftly, although two commissions on the same place in less than a year would certainly be a new record even for her.

It was now late February, so we were playing to a very tight ideal deadline if we wanted the house sold by early April. Ava raised her experienced eyebrows at the timing, especially with so many others struggling to sell in the very slow housing market on Prince Edward Island. As a professional, she had to be clear that she couldn't make any promises, but Ava didn't mind quietly hinting that she had a very good feeling about this. Darlington Gables was a well-known landmark in the area; a multi-gabled beauty on the crest of the hill where North Wiltshire met the Darlington Road. Approaching it from the south east, it made an incredibly impressive sight when viewed from the dip in the valley as the observer drove up towards the peak. Soon after we'd moved in, Andy had added to its distinctiveness with a seventy-five-metre-long shadowbox fence that took him a month to plan and another month to build. It was a very unusual feature for old–fashioned country houses on Prince Edward Island, and one of Andy's proudest achievements. Even he would admit that he was not generally very good at following through on goals, especially DIY projects. Now his magnificent fence and the house and my vegetable garden and our newly–planted fruit trees would be changing hands, almost as quickly as we'd embraced them.

Andy and I were clear that we wanted our home to be sold only to people we both had a very good feeling about. It just seemed like we owed the house that much, at least.

Within a couple of days, the following notice appeared in the local newspaper and on social media by the realtor on our behalf:

> *Are you looking for a country character home with ample living space for an incredible price? Look no further! This 5–bedroom, 3–bathroom home consists of many unique features, including high ceilings, detailed crown mouldings and original hardwood. This beautiful country home (15 minutes to Charlottetown) is a must–see! The house has a fantastic amount of space for your family to gather and create amazing memories. End your day watching the sun set over the countryside in the memorable sun–room and then relax in the whirlpool tub. Imagine hosting family gatherings around a warm fire, or next to a 9–foot Christmas tree. With a large eat–in country kitchen and a full–size dining room, you'll have plenty of room to host kitchen parties. The fully fenced in, private yard features numerous perennial flower beds, as well as peach, cherry, pear, blueberries, raspberries, and blackberries. There is a new large shed with a bay door to store your bikes and snowmobile – because the Confederation Trail is only seconds away. Don't miss out!*

As it happened, Darlington Gables was destined to sell far more quickly than even my optimistic longings could have ever anticipated. Within just six days, in fact, we rejected one offer for being laughably under our barest minimum figure, followed by a more reasonable offer from bidders who radiated goodwill and genuine interest in the property and its history. They were a retired couple from Ontario who were willing to dispense with the niceties and delays necessitated by an inspection, during which many old homes on the island would be found to need costly foundation work done including, no doubt,

Darlington Gables. This was in exchange for us moving out within three weeks and accepting fifteen percent less than our asking price. The offer was firm, with the bidders matter–of–factly stating upfront that they would not negotiate on price or terms. They'd been searching all over Nova Scotia and Prince Edward Island for the perfect home to retire to, and had identified a handful to choose from. Darlington Gables was by far their favourite, but they said they were willing to walk away.

Ava advised us to sit on the offer overnight. She was fairly sure that their take–it–or–leave–it approach was a bluff, but we had to decide for ourselves if it was worth the risk to counter offer or decline.

The offer really wasn't what we'd hoped for, quite frankly. Andy and I debated back and forth over dinner whether to submit a counter offer anyway to the couple from Ontario. Or should we turn it down, and risk the frustrations of waiting for another offer at what was traditionally a slow time of year in the island real estate market? On the other hand, the clock was ticking, and the proposed handover date was absolutely ideal for both of us.

Before the night was over, Andy texted Ava to let her know that we would go ahead and accept the offer.

Delighted for us, while sincerely hoping not to be selling Darlington Gables again any time soon, Ava got her husband to hammer in the sold sign through six inches of snow on the corner of our front lawn overlooking the valley highway. Once the paperwork was out of the way, she congratulated us on the speed of the sale with a great big hug and a large box of chocolates.

Everything now whirred into motion with urgent earnestness. In between frantic cleaning and packing and arranging the sale of household items that Andy didn't need, I began reaching out to international schools in Bratislava to find two spots for the boys for around mid–April. My own preference was for British English schools, which narrowed the choice down to a small handful. To my surprise, the first few schools I contacted – the bigger, more established institutions – had extensive waiting lists. I tried some of the smaller places too, only to hear the same story.

Just as I was beginning to consider American English schools after all, a Montessori kindergarten replied that yes, they had two spaces available and would be delighted to welcome Pat and Tom.. Reassured by the telephone interview I had with its director, and relieved by their lower fees compared to the bigger international schools, Andy and I decided to put the boys' names

WITH LOVE FROM BRATISLAVA   23

down there. I went ahead and took care of the paperwork, and ticked with relief that item off my to–do list.

The school now sorted, I turned my attention to where we were going to live. My inclination was to line up an apartment before we left. But Andy convinced me to stay at a hotel for the first few days and get a feel for the areas I felt comfortable in and then look around, rather than taking something I might later regret. Being patient when caught up in the middle of something I was excited about didn't come naturally to me, but I saw the wisdom in his advice, and ceded to common sense.

The date of the house sale was now rapidly approaching. The day before the handover, Andy, the kids, the cats, and I moved to a hotel on the outskirts of town, where we'd stay until the house funds came through. I could then buy our plane tickets, and Andy could begin looking for an apartment to rent unless or until the ideal house came on the market in the meantime.

Once the handover of Darlington Gables was complete and Ava confirmed everything was good to go, Andy and I met with our lawyer one last time to sign the deed over so that the funds could be released.

We weren't to know in this very modern day and age that our lawyer was a little traditional when it came to leveraging banking technology for financial transactions. To our astonishment, his assistant slid a separate envelope to both of us, with the words 'Cheque for House Sale Proceeds' alongside our individual names and the property address, typed with the unmistakeable tap–tappings of a good old–fashioned typewriter.

"Cheques?" Andy whispered a little too loudly to me, pulling out his slip of paper to verify the final balance after legal fees. "Who the heck still uses cheques?"

Overhearing this, the assistant shrugged her shoulders with resigned good humour. "We do all our banking with cheques."

The IT guy in Andy was not especially thrilled, but he was in no urgent need of the funds himself. He could wait for a few days. I, on the other hand, was horrified.

"How long will this take to clear?" I gasped. "I need to book our tickets as soon as possible. I have to put a deposit down with the kids' school to hold their places."

"They clear real quick. Usually five to seven days," the assistant assured me.

"Five to seven *what*? Why does it take that long?"

Shrug.

"Is it possible this one time to have the funds transferred to my bank account instead? Please? I've really got to get things going."

A reply in the patient negative was accompanied by a lecture on trust account procedures, fraud prevention measures, etc. In other words, there was nothing she could do.

Frustrated, I tried hard to reason with myself that the few extra days would go by anyway, whether I liked it or not. Eventually this would all be just a memory, right? In the meantime, I had more than enough to keep me distracted.

In the end, I waited seven excruciating days for the funds to clear before getting in touch with the central telephone banking number listed on the back of my deposit slip.

"I'm sorry," the banking representative informed me faux–cheerily. "Your cheque has been flagged for potential fraud. We've put a hold on it while we investigate. You'll have to contact our Fraud Department."

Why no one had bothered to inform me before now was beyond her script. With a polite apology, I was transferred to the Fraud Department.

After waiting on hold for more than five – yes, five – agonizing hours, forced to listen to the same three songs over and over again interspersed with "Please stay on the line. We are experiencing significant delays. Your call is important to us" until I was nearing the brink of insanity, the call was abruptly cut off. Beyond livid at the absolute waste of an afternoon, I had no choice but to start all over again through the central telephone banking number.

Reaching a different representative this time, I strongly insisted on being put through to someone else who could tell me what was going on with my cheque. The "Of course, let me see what I can do," was followed by a baffling roulette of internal transfers between various buck–passing departments before I inevitably found myself back on hold with the Fraud Department.

In sheer desperation, I decided to sort it out the island way. Andy drove me immediately into town where, with tears of outraged frustration, I breathlessly poured out the situation to the bank manager of my local branch. The various telephone departments had been emphatic that nothing could be done in person, and that a fraud hold must be investigated at a higher level through the federal Fraud Department. They obviously hadn't reckoned on the common sense of Prince Edward Island bank managers.

The manager snorted. "What *are* they talking about? So much has been centralised, but they haven't taken the power of intelligence away from us yet. I know the law firm you're talking about. They do things the old–fashioned way. I'm fine with authorising a lift on that hold."

She carefully reviewed the details on her computer, made a quick call to the lawyer's office, peered at her screen again, and tap–tapped at her keyboard.

"Done. You're good to go," the manager informed me with a smile.

Just. Like. That.

"Thank you so, so much," I cried, giving her a grateful hug.

"You're most welcome. Just hurry and book those tickets before our friends in the call centre get bored and put a stop on it again."

CHAPTER SIX

It was now mid–April, with all its nippy breezes and promising hints of spring proper a mere page–turn away.

The day of our departure had finally arrived. It was a wrench to leave the tranquillity and beauty of Prince Edward Island; the land of Anne of Green Gables and L.M. Montgomery; the province of potatoes and endless stretches of farmland and pistachio–green hills. I would miss the friends I'd made and the islanders I'd met through my food charity. To leave it all behind for an uncertain new chapter in life, therein lay the challenge.

People kept telling me that I was brave. Is that the word to define the fear of what might be if I didn't take this plunge? I certainly didn't feel very brave. Scared? Yes. A little crazy? Absolutely. Brave? Not so much.

We were to fly out from Moncton Airport, a provincial hub much bigger than Charlottetown, and with more frequent connections to Toronto and Montréal and then on to Europe. From Montréal, we would fly to Brussels, then to Vienna, and finally we'd get a taxi to Bratislava from there.

We had always enjoyed the drive across the grand stretches of the Confederation Bridge with its glimpses back to the red cliffs of the island and the rougher terrain of the New Brunswick coastline just up ahead. This time, though, the journey was at times full of chatter, at others uncertain silences, and always accompanied by the radio twittering away in the background, grasping at signals from island stations for as long as we could.

To the boys, this was the beginning of a fantastic adventure. They'd learned more about Europe through storybooks and videos and me, and Slovakia through Andy's tales of his time there as an English teacher. Now, with the promises of new types of sweets and a kindergarten that looked forward to welcoming them on Monday, Pat and Tom radiated cheerful curiosity about the journey. Although perhaps it was fair to say they were more immediately excited about their new little suitcases stuffed full of games and books.

Andy, with tears that would make themselves known, swiped the wetness away and repeated for the umpteenth time his promise to bring the kids more of their favourite toys as soon as we'd all settled in.

With many hugs for the boys and an awkward hug and kiss between me and Andy, we then were off through security and on our way to the gate.

I turned back one last time to give Andy a little smile of reassurance. He returned it with a nod that communicated his confidence in my ability to somehow make this work for us all. I could only hope that I wouldn't let him down.

One of the few obvious advantages of travelling with small children is boarding the plane ahead of everyone else. However, the journey that followed was long, very long, for me, and far too short for my excited little boys. With three flights to entertain them through, and absolutely determined as they were to not fall sleep until finally giving in mere hours from Brussels, it was my first exhausting hurdle in solo parenting.

The border guard at Brussels checked our documents carefully and then waved us through with a courteous welcome. Our flight had been forty minutes late, so I had to hurry the boys through to our connecting flight to Vienna, which would leave in less than an hour. I had a moment of concern over whether our bags would have time to be transferred to the flight, but I was too exhausted to overthink it. What would be, would simply just have to be.

The final leg of our air journey was smooth and thankfully caffeine–laden. When we arrived at Schwechat airport in Vienna, with our luggage safely retrieved from the baggage carousel, I manoeuvred the boys through to the arrivals hall and scanned the crowd for the taxi driver who was to take us to Bratislava.

"There, Mummy!" Tom pointed at a thin, grey–haired man holding a sign with my name on it in thick black marker pen.

The driver took one of the suitcases from me and led us through the exit that lay immediately ahead. He pointed to his black cab, just a few metres to the right. We made our way past the half–dozen smokers outside the main door, puffing away nervously at last–minute cigarettes before their flights.

Bags stowed, children buckled in, and a German language talk radio show on a setting just below blaring, the driver zipped us the sixty or so kilometres to Bratislava in just over thirty minutes. With Prince Edward Island drivers rarely afforded the luxury of going beyond ninety kilometres an hour – legally, anyway – the taxi's speed felt both exhilarating and terrifying.

It was a beautiful afternoon, and everything seemed even more alive in that glorious sunshine. Once beyond the outskirts of Vienna, the motorway eased itself into a gentle, precise countryside dotted with enormous wind turbines as far as the eye could see. I thrilled to the diversity of number plates that whizzed by us: Austrian, Slovak, Czech, Hungarian, German. Two lorries from Poland. A campervan from Switzerland. Even a motorbike from Ukraine.

I was *here*.

A few minutes later, we approached the blue–and–grey buildings that marked the Austrian–Slovak border. Random passport checks were being conducted by the Austrian *polizei* on vehicles entering their country; on the Slovak side, none.

The taxi drove straight over the border and, without any ceremony, we were in Slovakia.

The landscape changed almost immediately. The wind turbines were now behind us, replaced by green and chestnut fields waiting for the spring planting to begin. Signs above various overpasses gave the direction and distance to places such as Žilina, Brno, Budapest, Rusovce, and Jarovce.

Soon enough, we reached the sprawling mass of suburban Petržalka on the southern side of the Danube, before driving over the bridge into Bratislava proper.

"Look, Mummy, a UFO!" Pat cried, pointing up at a disc–shaped building atop the southern end of the bridge arch.

"Mummy, a castle, look!" Tom chimed in, bouncing up and down with delight. A little ahead to our left, up on a leafy crag on the north side of the river, a perfectly rectangular, whitewashed castle with four orderly medieval–style turrets stood, made more pristine still against the cheerful orange of the castle's roof.

We came off the bridge and drove by the semi–ruined stone walls of the old town, then onwards towards the forested hills above Bratislava. Before we knew it, our hotel came into view on the right just ahead. It was hard to miss with its creamy orange walls and huge blue soda company signs on the roof.

The hotel was really nothing fancy – more of a hostel than a proper hotel – but it was the closest accommodation to the Montessori that was available at short notice. Anyway, I was very tired, and very eager to change out of my nearly two–day–old clothes. I wasn't going to fuss.

Although it was late afternoon and only lunchtime back home, Tom and Pat were desperate for a nap. I paid the taxi driver and ushered the boys through the side door into the little reception area by the main stairs.

To my exhausted frustration, Pat chose this very moment to collapse in a fit of tired loud sobs on the floor. He was a dramatic child at the best of times, so you can imagine the scene. The cleaner hurried over to comfort him while I hastily checked in and paid for the room. She didn't speak a word of English, nor me Slovak aside from three words that Andy had taught me: *ahoj*, *prosím*, *d'akujem*. Hi, please, thank you. But Pat was content to nestle in her lap and enjoy the fuss while I gratefully took care of formalities. She then held Pat's hand and led him up the stairs while I lugged the suitcases, with Tom quietly trotting beside me.

Our room was very much on the spartan side. It reminded me of a student dormitory with its basic, low–fuss furnishings and bedding. But the curtains made a perfect seal against the late afternoon sunlight, and that was about all I really cared about at that specific little moment in time.

I got the boys quickly into their pyjamas, brushed their teeth and washed their faces, and threw on a pair of track pants and a shirt for myself. The three of us then cuddled up together in my bed, and fell swiftly asleep under the welcoming warmth of the white duvet.

CHAPTER SEVEN

The next morning was a bright and chilly Friday. Restless end–of–week traffic snaked briskly down the incline beyond the hotel towards the city centre, horns beeping and brakes slamming as drivers fiddled with their phones in the slipperiness of an unexpected mid–spring flurry.

Tom, Pat, and I hurried downstairs to the breakfast room, tummies rumbling. The server spoke no English, but she and I somehow muddled through with over–emphasised gestures and the staccato of one–word explanations as we negotiated breakfast.

We were quickly served with a large platter of supermarket–brand bread, packaged croissants, cheese, fruit, and meats. Nothing fancy, but very welcome all the same. Not being meat eaters, I piled up our plates with the rest of the platter and put the cold cuts aside. Despite complaining about not being that hungry, somehow the boys still managed to wolf down the contents of their own plates before attacking the remaining half of mine.

Once they'd finally had their fill, I took them by the hand and headed back up to our room to put on warm jumpers.

I'd pre–arranged to meet up with a friend of Ethan's, one of Andy's ex–colleagues. A real estate agent who spoke fluent English, Michaela Bieliková already had an apartment for me to view nearby.

We waited at the Magurská trolleybus stop, a 10–minute walk from the hotel. Soon enough, a smartly–dressed woman in her thirties stepped off the bus and caught my eye.

I recognised Michaela immediately from her picture on the agency's website, and gave a little wave. She strode over and shook my hand briskly, then said hello to the boys. We made small talk as Michaela fastened her green jacket against the flurry, and then followed her as she ushered us onto a particular bus.

Despite their jumpers, I felt guilty for not bundling the kids up as well as the Slovak children skipping on either side of the street with their parents.

A frigid gust dogged us as we got off the bus and hurried up the hill.

"You must have brought the Canadian spring with you," Michaela told the boys. "We usually get the last of our snow at the end of March, not now."

The four of us pushed against the wind, wet snowflakes slapping our cold faces, until we eventually came to a halt outside a semi–modern apartment building at the very top of a hill. It overlooked a leafy ravine, where people were out walking their dogs in spite of the weather.

The owner of the apartment was waiting outside for us, huddled in the doorway as the snow started up again in nippy earnest. He seemed surprised that I didn't speak Slovak, but made a polite effort at small talk in rusty English as the lift creaked upwards to the top floor.

It was a sparsely yet comfortably furnished two–bedroom apartment with a bathroom, living room, galley kitchen, and balcony. The style was very different to what we were used to in Canada, and definitely a lot smaller than the five–bedroom Darlington Gables. However, style was not my priority; what I wanted right now was a roof above our heads, so that the kids could get settled and roots could be planted.

The landlord explained to Michaela that he was a retired diplomat who had travelled extensively throughout his career. His son had lived in the apartment until fairly recently; in proof of this, his forgotten pot and bong were hastily hidden by his father as he showed us the living room and balcony.

After taking a good look around and feeling more than satisfied by the responses to my questions, I told them I'd take it. Michaela nodded, pleased at the speedy decision, and translated it to the owner to be absolutely sure of being understood.

He nodded, and we shook hands, and agreed to meet with Michaela on Monday to sign the contract and hand over the keys while the boys were at kindergarten. The landlord walked us all courteously to the lift, waved goodbye, and disappeared back into the apartment.

"That went well," Michaela declared with satisfaction. "What I'll do now is draw up the contract and get everything ready. He said he'll take care of getting beds for the boys over the weekend. I'll meet you back here on Monday to talk you through what you're signing, so you understand your obligations."

"Thank you so much. I can't believe it was so easy," I told her. "To be honest, I was torturing myself before I came here with all the things that could go wrong, seeing as I don't speak Slovak."

"Just relax. Everything will be fine. You'll see," Michaela reassured me. "Things are generally more complicated when you overthink them."

We parted back at the Magurská stop. Michaela got a trolleybus to her next appointment, while the boys and I walked back down the hill to our hotel. Along the way we stopped to pick up some groceries at a convenience store, where I was fascinated by two nuns in long habits shopping nonchalantly alongside a handful of teenage girls in bottom–hugging skirts, the latter oblivious to the weather.

The boys and I did a lot of exploring that first weekend. Once I figured out how to use the yellow ticket machines at most – but confusingly not all – public transport stops, we stocked up on a few tickets until I could find out how and where to buy monthly passes. Children under six travelled free, I soon discovered, so I only needed to take care of tickets for myself. At seventy cents per ticket, I marvelled at the cost compared to nearby Vienna, or even the rural bus service back on Prince Edward Island.

Conveniently, the 212 trolleybus passed very close to our hotel, and stopped at Hodžovo námestie in Staré Mesto, or the old town. After breakfast on Saturday, the boys and I jumped on the next one to come along, and took the four–minute journey with great excitement into town.

Tom and Pat listened with fascination to the miscellany of incomprehensible Slovak around them, particularly by other kids and their parents. It was their first puzzled realisation that English was no longer a language that would make them generally understood.

The trolleybus stop was located directly across from the white rococo presidential palace, with its oversized Slovak and EU flags flying in jaunty unison out front. Beyond the gates, a huge silver orb seemed to almost levitate in the very centre of a fountain, skirted by tourists and pigeons.

Clutching the boys by their hands, I guided them over one zebra crossing and then another, then down the road and over the tram tracks until we reached the entrance to old town proper. Michalská brána, or Michael's Gate, was barely visible from the modern roadway directly adjacent.

We walked through the barbican, the outer arched defence linked to a bridge that ran above the long–disappeared moat. We then came to a fourteenth century stone tower, a cheerful off–beige structure standing fifty metres tall, topped by a brass dome cupola tarnished turquoise over the centuries. We strolled under the arc leading into the cobbled Michalská Street, and merged with the throng of tourists ambling towards Hlavné námestie, the main square.

I felt the deepest, most grateful thrill to be alive and experiencing this moment in time. Forever more, no matter how long or short our stay here, I was giving the boys an experience that would forever be a part of them.

The square itself had retained so much of its Habsburg charm, despite the crowds and overpriced cafés and all the kitschy souvenir shops that went hand–in–hand with modern tourism. In the centre was a fountain, made up of an outer ring of light brown marble–effect slabs, which in turn contained a pool of limescale–green water which it collected and sprayed back out. In the very centre, ringed by a light–grey stone circle decorated with faces, the fountain was topped by a sixteenth–century statue of Maximillian II. Beyond the fountain was the town hall, a gothic complex of fourteenth and fifteenth century townhouses dominated by the lemon–shaded tower at their centre. Below the clock face, from a windy walkway wrapped narrowly around the upper tower, one could take in a splendid view over the old town below, and over towards the castle in the near distance. On all sides of the square were an attractive array of colourful buildings, each radiating the jaunty confidence of having witnessed and survived the assaults of history.

In other words, absolute bliss.

The boys, naturally enough, were more interested in the bronze statue of a Napoleonic soldier leaning coyly over one of the benches, eavesdropping on the conversations of whomever sat there. A nearby ice–cream stand and a take–away pizza shop completed their thumbs–up to Bratislava.

We spent the rest of that afternoon wandering from the old town to the nearby Eurovea shopping centre on the Danube to buy a mobile phone and a few groceries, before catching a bus back to the hotel.

By the time evening rolled around, Pat and Tom were, as can be imagined, thoroughly exhausted. After a quick shower, bedtime book, and chat with their father, they were out like two blown candles in their separate wooden beds.

Finally free to catch up on some work, I uncorked a bottle of wine and went through my backlog of client emails. I was high on adrenaline, nervousness, and exhilaration, not to mention anxious uncertainty, as I waited for the wine to take its medicinal effect.

My lap–top was still set to Prince Edward Island time, five hours behind Bratislava. As I stared at the old time in the bottom–right of my screen, I was almost painfully overwhelmed by the magnitude of what I'd just pulled off. The boys breathing heavily in their beds, their clothes and luggage and jackets in the corner, the very lap–top resting on the surface of the chipped laminate desk in the hotel room: all were real–time, unmistakable evidence of being here, and not there.

And, I – I was all alone. Aside from Michaela, I knew of no other soul in Bratislava.

With those odd quirks of sudden recollection that the brain is sometimes wont to produce, an ex–student suddenly sprang into my mind. As far as I could recall, he'd been the very first guest at our English language vacation business in Nova Scotia seven years ago. A young IT guy from Bratislava just three or four years younger than me, Ján had signed up for a two–week intensive course to improve his English. We'd got along well enough for me to keep in sporadic touch with him over the years, but it must have been three – four? – since we were last in contact.

Well, what's life without a little risk? If he didn't reply, at least I'd made the attempt. I looked up his Skype address and sent a brief message.

"It's your old English teacher here. I hope you haven't forgotten me! I'm now living in Bratislava. Small world! If you still live here and have time to catch up over a coffee sometime, feel free to let me know."

There. Sent.

Not ten minutes later, Ján messaged back with plenty of smiley face icons.

"Yes, I remember you! It's nice to hear from you. Why did you come to Bratislava? Of course, it is the best city in the world."

I smiled. I remembered how proud he was of his home town.

"Just needed a change of scenery. Andy and I separated – it's all good. I just wanted to come back to Europe, and to give the kids a chance to experience international life. By the way, I have two kids now: Tom (I think I told you about him? He was born the year after you visited us. He's nearly five–and–a–half) and Pat (just turned four)."

"Wow! When did you arrive?"

"Thursday."

"Thursday! So you just got here. Great! We can meet up on Wednesday if you would like."

"Sure! During the day works best for me. The kids will go to a Montessori near Koliba, so I can meet anytime up till mid–afternoon, say 2.30pm."

"Great! I'll send you a message on Tuesday to agree where we can meet. I look forward to seeing you again. I hope you'll understand my poor English."

"Ha ha. You're doing OK so far. I look forward to it, too!"

I suddenly felt just a teensy bit less alone. Also, slightly tipsy – the wine was hitting my tired head faster than usual. I definitely didn't want a hangover while out–and–about with the kids tomorrow. So, I put away the wine, and switched on the kettle.

The rest of the evening was devoted to clearing my work emails and getting my to–do list back into some sort of order.

Sunday was very much like Saturday: exploring and eating and getting a feel for our new home. I found out about an indoor playground just a short bus ride away, and took the boys there for a few hours to hang out with some other children and work off some energy. Kids being kids, none of them cared who spoke what language. They had a thoroughly fabulous time.

"Mummy," Tom exclaimed as he ran by, catching my hand in his sweaty fingers.

"Yes, my baby?"

"I love Slovakia!"

I grinned. "Because of the indoor playgrounds?"

Tom nodded solemnly. "They're much funner here!"

I stared after him as he dashed over to the other kids, hauling tire tubes up to the top of the indoor toboggan track and hurling themselves down with loud squeals. Tears of pride sprang into my eyes. Tom was my sweet, golden–haired little boy with his calm nature, his smarts for numbers, his instinctive competitiveness. A vivid personality contrast to Pat, with his loud explosions of joy or sorrow, his innate mischievousness, and his bafflingly short attention span when it came to doing what he was told.

I was awed by their openness and adaptability. As guilty as I felt about taking them away from their father, both Andy and I knew that they would be fine.

So far, we were absolutely right.

CHAPTER EIGHT

At 11.30am on Monday, just as I was about to check out of the hotel, my new phone rang. It was Michaela.

"I just got off the phone with the owner of the apartment. Unfortunately, it's not good news. He can't meet today. I'm really sorry."

"What, why?" I exclaimed. "I was just heading over there!"

Michaela sighed uncomfortably. "He says he's sick. He's also saying that he really doesn't want the address to be registered with the alien police, which it'd have to be because you need that information in the contract when you go to the police."

"What's the point, if I can't register the address I'm living at, which I'm legally obliged to do? He said he was OK with it when we met."

"I know. But he's having second thoughts."

"So what he's saying is, he prefers a Slovak?"

Michaela was silent on the other end.

"Damn. I thought he was a diplomat?" I continued in a panic. "Aren't diplomats supposed to be open–minded and welcoming of other cultures?"

"I know, I know. It's really stupid. He's being super cautious. But do you really want to rent from someone who thinks like that? It's good we found out now. Right?"

I knew I'd probably agree one day, but right now I was too stressed by this last–minute thunderbolt to think in such forgiving terms. This meant that I had to find somewhere else, and quickly. In the meantime, I needed to book another hotel. The boys would finish their first day at the Montessori in just over three hours. The morning receptionist had already mentioned the hotel was fully booked that night, so we literally had nowhere else to stay.

As soon as Michaela hung up, I pulled out my lap–top and urgently scrolled through the major travel sites to find an option, any option. I didn't care if we had to share a bed or stay in a bedsit a few miles out of town. We needed a roof over our heads tonight while I sorted this mess out.

Sold out. No rooms left. Nothing available. Zilch, nada, nicht.

On and on I scrolled, each listing declaring the same frustrating story. Desperately, I pulled up one more site and skimmed hastily through their listings. Finally, a possible option, right in the heart of Staré Mesto. It was a holiday apartment rather than a hotel, and the price was a little outside my budget, but I was willing to take just about anything right now.

I dialled the number, fingers sweating. Please, please, please, I silently begged.

Within three rings, a lady identifying herself as Vilma picked up the phone. Yes, she spoke English. Yes, she owned Welcome City Cottages. Yes, they had a vacancy for a week. Yes, it was available today. Someone had cancelled at the last moment because of a family emergency, so an apartment with a double bed and a sofa bed was available immediately.

Overjoyed with relief, I rattled out my story and the sudden predicament I now found myself in.

Vilma made little exclamations of surprise as she listened. She quickly assured me that the apartment was most definitely available for the week, and we were very welcome to rent it longer if need be while I searched for a more permanent solution. Vilma confirmed the price and the address, and informed me that her nephew would meet me there in an hour.

Propelled by adrenaline, I hung up and checked out of the hotel as hastily as possible.

As I travelled into town on the 212, I peered at the crumpled tourist map that the receptionist had given me. The street I was heading to was completely unfamiliar. Anytime I looked up for the merest nanosecond, my finger would somehow slip, and I had to pinpoint it on the map all over again.

I got off at Hodžovo námestie as Vilma had instructed. I weaved through the throng of passengers getting off or jumping on to the red trolleybuses, sweatily dragging the suitcases along as best I could. I know, I know, a taxi would have been so much simpler. But I hadn't wanted to sacrifice precious time to find an English–speaking driver.

I made my way to the underpass outside the presidential palace, down the stairs, through the concourse to the left, up the escalator on the other side, and into the square. Within a minute I was on the pedestrianised Obchodná Street, Bratislava's main shopping thoroughfare. Double–checking the map to make sure I was heading in the right direction, I continued on past Kamenné námestie with all its bustle of pedestrians and restaurants before realising I'd gone too far. I turned back and retraced my steps a little, dragging those damn suitcases behind me. A short passageway soon took me close to where the map and my senses told me the holiday apartment should be. I won't divulge exactly where it was, but suffice to say, I found it soon enough.

There, waiting at the entrance to a little courtyard overlooked by several numberless tourist apartments, was a tall, well–dressed man in his fifties with white hair, oily cheeks, and a friendly expression.

"Mr. Zubercov?"

"Dušan. You are very welcome."

I sighed my thanks as he relieved me of the largest suitcase, its handle glistening with my sweat. Pulling the other behind me while lugging the boys' backpacks over one arm, I followed Dušan as he led me up six tiled outer steps to the apartment I would be staying in.

Dušan jiggled and rocked the key a little. "I must have this fixed," he muttered. "The guest before you was too strong with it." He twisted again, pulling it slightly towards him, and the key turned. The door swung open with a slight shriek, a sound more intriguing that off–putting. Dušan went in a step ahead of me, wheeling the suitcase into a corner. I propped the smaller suitcase against it, and dropped the backpacks nearby in a heap.

"My aunt told me your story. I'm sorry. Please believe, foreigners are very welcome in Slovakia."

"Thank you. I don't think he was against foreigners, don't get me wrong. He seemed nervous about the contract and the police. It was just unfair that he seemed to change his mind at the very last moment."

Dušan shook his head. "How long would you stay here for?"

"In Bratislava, at least a year. Here, a week if that's OK. Hopefully I'll find an apartment quickly. I need to get the kids settled. But I have someone helping me with that."

My phone rang at that moment. Dušan nodded his willingness for me to interrupt our discussion to answer it.

"Good news," Michaela immediately informed me. "He's changed his mind. He said he'll add that clause. He's feeling a little better if you want to stop by at four o'clock to sign the contract."

I stared at the ceiling, and shook my head.

"I found a holiday apartment to rent for the week because of all this. I'm busy with the owner right now. I've got all my stuff here. I don't want to move it all again."

"But he's changed his mind. It's what you wanted, isn't it?"

"Yes, but I don't appreciate him doing this. How do I know he won't change his mind again? I'm sorry, I think it's best to pass."

"So, you're not going to take it then?" I could hear the crossness in Michaela's voice.

"No, sorry. He's unreliable. I've got my kids to think of; I can't have that. If you can help me find somewhere else, that would be great. If I find somewhere else in the meantime, I'll definitely come to you. I want you to get your commission."

We hung up so that Michaela could go and break the news to the owner.

"Sorry about that," I apologised to Dušan.

Deep in thought, he nodded distractedly. Then, "Please, one moment. I will call my aunt. It may be that we can help."

While Dušan spoke with Vilma, I took a closer look at the rooms. The apartment was very compact, and decorated in what I figured was an older Slovak style. As advertised, it came with a table and four chairs, a double bed and sofa bed, a kitchen full of utensils, and – unadvertised but proudly displayed – a prominent wooden crucifix in the little vestibule between the outer and inner door. Despite a slight hint of mustiness, it was perfect for a week or so.

"Please, my aunt would like to talk to you," Dušan called out from the living room.

I returned to the front room and took the phone from his outstretched hand.

"She is more fluent than I," Dušan explained. "I have it on speaker so we can all hear very good."

"Hello, this is Vilma. You are very welcome."

"Thank you – and thank you again for taking us at such short notice."

"Oh, it is our big pleasure. Would you do something for us?"

"Of course."

"We would like to make you feel welcome after your experience. We don't treat foreigners like that. You are our business. We would like you to consider staying with us."

"Staying?"

"What I mean is, to rent our apartment. We've rented it for a long time many times before. We rented to an American diplomat not so long ago. We rented it to a Canadian lady before him, but she was not as grateful as she should have been. She gave my nephew a lot of difficulty."

Dušan looked distinctly uncomfortable at the recollection. He didn't strike me as the type to willingly stand up to strong personalities. He seemed very much under Vilma's thumb.

"But we have a good feeling about you," his aunt continued, "and we feel very sorry for your experience. Dušan is very impressed with your attitude. We can rent it for the same rate you were going to pay the owner, if that is convenient to you."

I thought quickly. Although the unit was a bit small and old–fashioned, the location was absolutely perfect, right in the heart of the old town. It was a slight trek to get the kids to and from school, admittedly, but the bus connections were very good. I had to find somewhere rapidly so I could get our applications for temporary residency submitted to the alien police, so it wasn't like I had much choice. Anyway, I reasoned, if things didn't work out, I could always find somewhere else later on. Dušan and Vilma seemed like genuine people, and they were certainly saying all the right things. The fact that they spoke English was also a definite advantage.

"OK. Yes. Yes, I'm interested," I told them. "If you can draw up the contract as soon as possible – in the next couple of days – I'll have my realtor take a look. It's my first time dealing with the paperwork here, so I'll hand everything over to her. Thank you for your offer. I really appreciate this."

"Feel welcome! Please can you give the phone back to Dušan?"

I did so, and listened with relieved curiosity as they discussed the particulars in Slovak.

Dušan hung up, smiled at me, and kindly stroked my flushed cheek.

"You are safe here now. We welcome you and your children. Your husband, will he visit?"

"Yes, sometimes. I'll probably take the boys back to visit him in a few weeks, or he'll come here. We're still figuring it out."

We stood up and shook hands. Dušan took note of Michaela's contact details so he could forward her the necessary documentation, gave me a quick hug, repeated their warm welcome, and hurried on with long strides through the courtyard.

I felt a little stunned by how quickly everything had about–faced in the space of just two hours. I most definitely looked forward to soothing my nerves with a glass or three of wine after the kids had gone to bed, that's for sure.

CHAPTER NINE

With Michaela, Vilma, and Dušan working on the rental agreement, I focused on getting the rest of the alien police paperwork together. I'd already lost a few precious days thanks to the first landlord. Everything needed to go smoothly from here on to make up for the lost time.

As suggested in his email, I met Pavel Hacek at Café Dias, close to the Hodžovo námestie underpass.

When I had originally looked through the police registration requirements, it all seemed fairly straightforward, if heavy on the paperwork. But Slovakia wasn't the first country I'd moved to with a long list of documents to produce. However, after reading one too many horror stories online about actually dealing with the alien police here, I knew there was no way I could do this on my own, at least the first time. Especially with people saying that the alien police were forbidden to speak English.

The most popular route seemed to be to hire an immigration specialist. I put up a post on an expat forum to ask for current recommendations.

Within minutes, one of the more active members sent me a message. He forwarded the contact details for his cousin, a lawyer–turned–immigration–consultant. The best possible combination for dealing with the alien police, he enthused. This cousin mostly worked with Russian corporate clients, he told me, but was fluent in English and was currently taking on new individual clients. Impressed by the background information and website link that he sent me, I went ahead and contacted the cousin. I was further assured by the speed of his reply in good English, and arranged a meeting for the very next day.

It was around mid–morning, and the café's atmosphere was relaxed: the calm before the lunch–time rush. Pavel gestured towards a little table at the back. Once seated, we ordered coffee from the server, who was trying to recover from a fit of giggles at a colleague accidentally spilling an espresso down her shirt.

"Thank you so much for meeting with me."

Pavel nodded, and flipped open his leather notebook. He was handsome in a run–down sort of way. He had the appearance of a serial all–night video gamer, and the aftershave tastes of a teenager. He was dressed professionally in a dark grey suit, with his jacket left open in deliberate business casual style.

I quickly launched into a summary of my background and first few days in Bratislava, the sort of work I hoped to pursue, and the type of visa I preferred to apply for.

Pavel listened, took down some notes, and nodded some more. "If you have success here, it is better to create a company," he advised, once I finally stopped talking.

"Yes, I read about that. I also read that a lot of entrepreneurs doing my sort of work start with a sole trader licence and see how things go. As I just moved here and I'm not sure how long I'll stay, I figure the sole trader option is best for now. The advantage is, that also frees up my savings because I won't need to invest so much."

"If you earn more than eight hundred euro a month, a company is better for tax purposes."

"I don't know how much I can earn right now, to be honest. Of course, I hope I do well, but it's all so new. I spoke to a few ex–colleagues of my husband's; they've all been here for at least eight or ten years. All except one of them has a sole trader license. That guy runs his own language school. When my visa expires, and if I stay longer, I'll consider going down the company route at that point."

Pavel gave a tiny nod, and moved on.

"You will also need a registered business address."

"Oh, so I can't use my home address?"

"No. In Slovak law, your home address and business address must be separate."

"But I'll work from home. What should I do?"

"I have an agreement with a hotel in Staré Mesto for my clients to use as a business address. It is very easy to arrange."

"Wonderful, thank you. What's the cost?"

"My fee is €249 to set the hotel agreement up for one year. The hotel asks you to book a room for minimum ten days for each person, each year. But it must be paid at the beginning, to use it for a legal address. For you and your children, the cost for ten days would be," he double–checked on his phone calculator, "€917, and my fee. €1166 total."

I was horrified. "Um, are there any other options?"

Pavel shook his head. "It's possible, but I don't know. My clients usually contact me before they arrive, so they need hotel. This is simpler."

"OK, thank you. I'll have a think about it and get back to you as soon as possible."

Pavel said nothing as he scrawled another note. I got the feeling my attractiveness as a client had dropped dramatically during this short conversation. Well it was my money, I reminded myself, and I had to protect it. Bratislava may have a lower cost of living than, say, nearby Vienna, but this was the first time in years that I couldn't fall back on two incomes.

With me clear on what I'd like to do, Pavel gave a quick overview of the steps to be taken: secure a personal and business address, apply for a sole trader license, register with the tax office, apply for temporary residency permits through the alien police, sign up for public health insurance for myself and the children, and get medicals. All in Slovak. I was very grateful for Pavel's service, even if he seemed less than enthused by my lower commission value. However, if I did become successful, it was in his best interests to provide excellent service.

Pavel confirmed that he'd put together the necessary paperwork to be completed. He would also get in touch with Michaela to introduce himself and check on the progress of the rental agreement. Once everything was ready, we'd meet up again to sign the documents and pay the fees.

Delighted at everything beginning to get underway, I shook hands with Pavel, paid for our coffees, and we parted ways outside the café.

CHAPTER TEN

The next morning, with the kids off to Montessori and our suitcases unpacked, I took time out to explore my new surroundings before meeting up with Ján at Kollárovo námestie.

I walked down busy Obchodná Street with its myriad of clothing stores and take–aways and stationers and cafés, doing my best to figure out what the menu boards outside some of the restaurants said. I could still remember a bit of Polish and Ukrainian, both of which had similarities to Slovak, but I couldn't make heads nor tails of the words. As always, it would come in time, I told myself.

Towards the end of Obchodná before it met Kollárovo námestie, I spotted a small sliding glass window in a non–descript orange wall. It was not particularly noticeable unless you happened to walk by. Above the window was a dark blue awning with the word PIRÔŽKY announcing its sole culinary offering in white capital letters. I later learned that it was a decades–old landmark on the street, its popularity cheerfully unaffected by the recent explosion of restaurants and cafés, the rise and fall of communism, or dietary fads.

Within lay a small counter, where a woman with dark hair and a bright smile rapidly served the non–stop wave of customers who sidled up to her window and quietly muttered their requests. A yellow checkered curtain formed a makeshift wall immediately behind her. She spoke very little English, but one raised finger and a poorly–accented "Um… pirôžky, po prosím" were readily understood.

Fifty cents and ten seconds later, I took the warm plastic bag she handed me, slid it down just so, and bit into the fried brioche–like batter of the hand–length pirôžky baton. Its subtle sweetness and deep–fried deliciousness were heavenly, the cottage cheese within both stodgy and surprisingly tasty. The grease of the Pirôžky's brief deep–fry gathered in an uneven stain on the serviette beneath, glossing my fingers tantalisingly in spite of the bag.

As I doubled back towards the old town with the remnants of my pirôžky, I came across a coffee stand, or "one of those hipster wagons" as Michaela had grimaced when we had passed by one on the previous Friday. A white canvas sign affixed to the side of the wagon sported a picture of a man with rabbit ears and whiskers, holding a banner which said "Pán Králiček". Mr Rabbit.

The English–speaking tourist in front of me was attempting to order coffee in Slovak with the help of a phrase list in the back of her little guide book. The tall, bearded barista smiled politely, his eyes twinkling at her pronunciations. He let the lady finish her sentence before informing her in perfect English that he spoke perfect English. With a relieved giggle, the tourist paid for her flat white and manoeuvred her backpack–laden shoulders out of sight.

"I warn you, my Slovak is even worse than that," I greeted him.

"Worse? Impossible!" he laughed. "What would you like?"

"A small latte, please."

"*Malé latte.* Of course."

Like an elegant bear, I watched him expertly grind and tamp the coffee, and brew it into an espresso. He then deftly stood aside to release the steam from the wand once he'd heated and aerated the milk. He gently swirled the pitcher and lightly tapped the bottom against the counter to get rid of any remaining bubbles. Then, quickly and assuredly, he swirled the glossy white liquid in circular motions on top of the dark espresso; pausing mid–way to let the milk settle for a moment. He finished off by forming a flower pattern on top of the foam, and handed me the cup.

"I've given up trying to do butterflies," he grinned, as I took the latte from him and handed over some coins. "How long are you in town for?"

"Actually, I just moved here. For at least a year, probably longer. I haven't decided yet."

"Good choice. Bratislava is a very interesting place. Small, but interesting."

"Yes. So far, I fully agree about the interesting part."

"Well, good luck. Oskar," he held out a large hand, "We do the best coffee in Bratislava, just so you know. Stop by and get another *malé* latte some time. Here, take a customer loyalty card."

I shook his hand and put the card in my bag. His hand was strong and muscular, warm and friendly.

"Thank you. I will for sure."

As I walked away, I nodded and smiled at the presumably–homeless guy who'd been listening with great interest to our conversation. Sitting perfectly upright in the fold–up chair provided by Oskar, with his tattered suitcase and a shopping bag of possessions tucked underneath, he ran his fingers through his long grey hair and gave me a finger tap salute on his temple in return.

I sipped the latte, closing my eyes for a moment as I savoured the comforting pleasure that only good coffee can give. It really was excellent, just as Oskar had promised.

As it was suddenly close to midday, I made my way back towards Kollárovo námestie again, ignoring the nearly–irresistible pirôžky window on the corner.

Ján hadn't specified which side of the square to meet him on, and I hadn't thought to check. Trolleybuses or trams stopped on all sides, with the view between obscured by tall trees and an unruly plethora of hedges around the square.

But I needn't have worried. Ján was easy to spot with his unmistakable height, close–trimmed beard, and confident pink shirt. He was waiting in the middle of the square, phone in hand in case I texted to say that I was lost or delayed.

We kissed in European style on both cheeks.

"You haven't changed a bit," I told him. "It's also nice that you somehow knew to colour–coordinate your shirt with my dress."

Ján smiled. "What can I say, I have a talent."

First things first: where to go for coffee. The square was home to a huge international company, so it was more a case of finding a place that wasn't crowded with office workers.

"Hipsters," Ján corrected me.

I smiled. "One of my new acquaintances here uses that term as well."

"They're everywhere in Bratislava. Five, ten years ago, you couldn't get a latte. Now, everyone drinks them."

We scurried across a busy road and turned onto Józefská Street, where we took a seat inside one of Ján's favourite cafés, Randevú.

"Espresso," he told the server. "What will you have?"

"Um, a latte please," I replied sheepishly.

The café was decorated in a relaxed, would–be–minimalist style. Bookshelves and cushions broke up the clean lines and added splashes of colour to offset the muted shades of the tan walls, blackboard wall menus, and horizontal stone tiles lining the façade of the bar.

"Forgive me if I'm wrong, but isn't this place the very definition of hipster?" I asked mischievously, as the server brought us our orders.

Ján pretended not to hear me. "I should take you some time to a café here owned by a Canadian guy, Ben. It's called Next Apache. I've been there a few times. The walls are full of books in English."

"Apache, like, the Indian tribes?"

"Yes, exactly. When he first came to Slovakia, he heard the expression *nech sa páči* and thought we were saying 'next apache'. When he opened his café, this is what he called it."

"Clever."

Ján nodded, smiling.

We sipped our coffees, me more slowly than him. Don't get me wrong, I loved coffee, but I didn't usually drink more than one or two in a day. I was beginning to get a slight headrush after the amount I'd already consumed that morning.

"When's the last time you spoke English?" I asked, making conversation.

"I think, not since I stayed with you and Andy in Canada. Mostly, I use Slovak or German. My English is not very good anymore. You can hear that I've forgotten a lot of words."

"Yes, your English is very bad indeed. No one could possibly understand you," I smirked. "It's funny, I was thinking the other day of a time when you really demonstrated your flexibility in English. Do you remember the lesson we had, when you forgot the word for suitcase? I told you what it was in German and you wouldn't believe me, because you'd forgotten it in German, too. I don't know how the whole thing turned into an argument, but it did. I remember shaking with anger and thinking you were the most impossibly frustrating student I'd ever worked with. Then when you realised it was actually *koffer*, you were very much the gentleman when you agreed you were mistaken. I believe we even shook hands over it at the end of the class."

"Hmm, I don't remember that."

"Oh, I'll never forget it. It was quite funny, really. Later, when I wasn't so cross. We got over it, and everything went smoothly for the rest of your stay. And so, are you still working in IT?"

"Yes. I have three regular clients. I should get some more, but I like sleeping too much."

I laughed.

"It's true. My clients don't contact me before eleven. They gave up," he grinned. "I like staying awake late more than waking early. It's better for me. I'm a night…"

"Owl."

"Yes. Unfortunately, most offices are closed when I like to work. So, I must have more clients and less sleep, or not so many clients and more sleep. I choose the freedom to be poor."

"Fair enough. You have no wife, no kids – you're a free man. No one to nag you."

Ján smiled. "So, you are in Bratislava now. Tell me the story."

I was happy to oblige. We ended up staying in the café for over an hour, catching up on our lives over the past few years. Ján gave me some tips about kid–friendly activities to do in Bratislava, and promised to send me some recommendations about places to eat.

After paying for our second round of coffee, Ján walked me back to the apartment.

I'd really enjoyed seeing him again. He was very easy to talk to, and seemed to be interested in a wide variety of topics. It also gave me a degree of reassurance that someone I knew wasn't too far away should I ever need to reach out for help.

CHAPTER ELEVEN

"Remind me: what documents do you need for the alien police?"

Following my latest meeting with Pavel, I got in touch with Michaela to discuss the specifics of the rental agreement. It appeared to be one of the trickiest documents that people online had complained about after going to the alien police. Some of them had been sent away to redo the agreement altogether, or to change the wording. The details had to be precise, so I wasn't taking any chances.

Pavel had given me the list of application requirements in Slovak and slightly confusing English. I emailed it over to Michaela while we chatted on the phone.

Although the draft contract was ready to go, it now seemed that it wasn't enough according to Pavel's list. There were certain supporting documents required to verify its legal validity in the eyes of the alien police, despite it being a legal agreement in itself. Michaela stopped me several times to clarify what Pavel had said about particular points, taking careful notes before reading a summary back to me.

"And what about the *katastra* confirmation, does it need to be the official version, or the free version you can just download off the internet?"

"He said he usually takes the internet version."

"That's strange. They were very strict when my boyfriend went through the process a few years ago. But OK, that's why I wanted to check – I guess things have changed," she shrugged. "Good. The internet version is easier, anyway. What about the rental agreement then, what needs to go in there again? I just want to make sure we've got everything covered in this draft. It'd be painful to start all over."

"Pavel said we just need to include my full name, the start and end dates, and importantly, the clause stating I can use the address for the purpose of registering for residency in Slovakia. Similar to the contract you drafted for the other place. As the *katastra* document is the proof of property ownership, he said we need to submit that also to the alien police with the agreement.

"OK. Did Pavel say if anything else needs to be notarised, or…?"

"He said 'Possibly'."

"Do you think that's a yes or a no?"

"He said it really depends."

"On?"

"To quote Pavel, 'One officer says one thing, another says something else. I usually just try and if they ask us to come back, we come back'."

Michaela muttered something under her breath about hourly rates. "Maybe it's easier when you're a rich Russian client. In this case, you're most definitely not. OK, so I'm going to give you the original of the rental agreement when I'm done. Better we do the changes now than get the wrong officer. We should meet up with Vilma and Dušan to sign it, then go to the notary. I'll get in touch with Pán Hacek in case of any questions, so we can make sure everything is in order before you go to the alien police. Good?"

"Perfect. Thank you so much."

"Not at all. You can get me one of those hipster coffees sometime."

I smiled in willing agreement.

Michaela, Vilma, Dušan, and I sat on the dark leather sofa and wooden chairs in the cramped sitting room of my new apartment. The sun beamed through the teal–and–mandarin curtained windows, while the pigeons oh–oo–ooed softly on the dilapidated roof of the building directly across the courtyard.

Michaela had an appointment with a nearby client in twenty minutes, so she quickly kicked off the formalities.

"Two copies of the contract, two copies of the inventory," she informed us all, placing the duplicate documents down on the wooden coffee table. "They're prepared in Slovak and English. You've all seen the drafts in your email, so there should be no need for further corrections. Please read through them again, and sign at the bottom of each copy of the contract. Also, the inventory."

Dušan, Vilma, and I scrutinised our hard copies and signed where indicated. Michaela then nodded at the envelope in my lap. I unsealed it and counted out the first month's rent, the first three months' utilities, and the deposit in front of them all, one crisp note at a time.

I handed the pile of notes over with more than a touch of quiet irritation. Only after the draft rental agreement was emailed across did I realise that Vilma had seemingly misunderstood our verbal and written communications. The first apartment I'd looked at with Michaela was a full–size, 2–bedroom property, with all utilities included for €900.

Without thinking, I had revealed the rate to Vilma, who had offered me her apartment "at the same rate" beforehand. She had taken a gamble, hoping that what I was going to pay for the original apartment was higher than she would ordinarily charge for this apartment. It didn't occur to me that I'd revealed the figure without making any provision to negotiate, given the much smaller size of Vilma's apartment, until the draft was sent out. When I had then reviewed it, I was even more astonished to see the rent set at €900 *plus* an additional €90 per month for utilities. Vilma had somehow forgotten that the agreed rate was inclusive, even though I had it in writing in one of our numerous emails. Despite Michaela's intervention, she would only reduce the utilities to €80 as a gesture of goodwill. I desperately needed somewhere to stay, as they well knew, so I felt myself cornered into losing that battle to win the war.

"€900 rent, €900 deposit, plus €240 for the first three months' utilities," Michaela confirmed. She watched carefully as Vilma and Dušan signed the receipt, and then handed signed copies of the agreement to both parties and the receipt to me. She gathered her things and stood up.

"Sorry to rush off," Michaela apologised. "It's the only time the seller and this potential buyer are available to meet. The owner goes on vacation this Saturday." She grabbed her bag and documents, shook hands all round, and hurried through the vestibule to the courtyard outside, promising to call me later.

The instant Michaela closed the door, Vilma and Dušan looked at each other and then at me.

"I would like to ask you a very big favour," said Vilma. "Would you do that for us?"

"If it's possible, I'm sure I can do it," was my cautious reply.

"It is easier for us if you pay €500 to my bank account, and the rest in cash every month."

"Oh, OK?"

"It's easier, because there are two of us, you see. You can put the €500 in my account, and give Dušan the remaining cash on the twenty–first of each month. He will give you a receipt, of course."

"I don't *think* I see any problem with that."

Vilma seemed relieved. She smoothed down her greying hair and glanced at her nephew.

"Thank you. Dušan will print a new copy of our contract and bring it to you this afternoon. There's no need to tell Michaela; we already have a contract, so we just need to edit the amount. It's better to just have €500 on the official contract. The government doesn't like rent paid in cash, even if the reason is very innocent. But this arrangement is much easier for us. I travel much, so I won't always be here when rent is due."

"I'm sorry to ask, but is this going to affect the terms of my agreement? I need this for my alien police application."

"Not at all. Everything is exactly the same; just the amount is different on the paper. To thank you, we would like to offer you a discount on your utilities, €60 not €80. Yes? It really is a great convenience for us if we do it this way. With my travels, it's better for Dušan to collect his amount directly from you. He is always around. You will be happy to do that for us, yes?"

Vilma gazed across at me so pleasantly, so hopefully, emanating such effortless goodwill and above–boardedness, that I acquiesced despite my misgivings. So long as it didn't affect me in any way, I was willing to not overthink it. Things were done differently here, I told myself.

"Thank you," Vilma beamed, shaking my hand. "Dušan will come back with the updated copies very soon."

In less than an hour the doorbell buzzed again, announcing a visitor with a tinny *praaaap*. At the top of the stairs was Dušan, with his very long legs and genial smile, back promptly as Vilma had promised.

His aunt was not able to meet with us again that day, as her elderly mother needed someone to take her grocery shopping.

Dušan took off his sizeable leather shoes and sat down on the sofa, legs twisted awkwardly against the low height of the coffee table. He had brought with him two copies of the agreement signed by himself and his aunt, freshly updated with the new on–paper rent.

I quickly flicked through each version to be certain there were no other changes, then signed both at *Podpis / Nájomník* and gave one copy back to Dušan.

"Thank you," he nodded, placing it on the sofa beside him. "And, are you, you are comfortable here?"

"Yes. Thank you to you both for your kindness. The location is great, by the way – so close to the bus and for shopping."

"Good. We are happy. Before, we had many people stay here. Many very nice, some not so nice. Some guys from Middle East, or Africa, I don't know where. Ah, we did not like them so much. We have a rule, take shoes off, and leave shoes at the beginning... no, not beginning. Entrance. We want the floor – the carpet, rug? – to not get old for many years. No shoes, just socks. This is fair, I think, yes? But these men, they did not like this, they do not do this in their country, so they refused. They understood, but they would not agree."

"I'm sorry to hear that. But, so far so good for us, and I'm sure I'll have nothing to complain about. You've both been wonderful."

"Thank you. Now I will go. If you need anything more for the police, please let us know. We signed documents for another visitor, three maybe four years before now. The police can be very difficult, I know. I do not understand this. The government lets in too many refugees and people without documents, but they make it very difficult for people like you."

I didn't much like this attitude, but I kept my thoughts to myself. From what I knew, Slovakia wasn't used to taking in refugees. Sixteen the year before, which was an increase of one over the year before that, according to Andy. It was hardly what I'd call an influx.

"I've found myself an immigration lawyer, so everything should be fine. Thank you for your kindness. I'll be sure to let you know."

Dušan leaned forward. "It is a pleasure for me to talk to someone like you. Some of the people before, ah. I have told you some stories. I am a 'people person' – this is the correct expression, yes? – as I think I have heard it in English. I like friendly people."

He stroked my cheek again, just like he did the first time we met. I couldn't help but pull away a little, despite his innocent intentions. I was a touchy–feely type myself, but not with complete strangers. I'd have to get used to this Slovak demonstrativeness.

Dušan wasn't offended by my hesitation, however. He shook my hand warmly, folded his copy of the agreement under one arm, and left me to do a quick bit of work before I had to collect Pat and Tom from Montessori.

CHAPTER TWELVE

Three days before we were due to go to the alien police in Petržalka to submit our applications, I sat down one more time with Pavel at Café Dias to go over the final details. After handing over his exorbitant fee, I gave Pavel everything I'd collected since our previous meeting, including the updated rental agreement.

I sipped on my latte as he flicked through the documents.

"Where is your husband's permission?"

"My husband's what?"

"This separation agreement from Canada, it's not enough. It must be in Slovak."

I was puzzled. "We've been through everything already, twice. It's the first time I've heard this."

Pavel, focused on the paperwork, didn't look up. "We don't have a separated status in Slovakia. You need a notarised letter from your husband, in Slovak, with very specific wording. The police may reject it anyway, but it must be included. I will prepare the document for your husband to sign. His lawyer must notarise his signature. That is very important. I need it by the evening before we go to the police."

"But Pavel, how am I supposed to get it back here in two days? It's impossible."

He stared at me for a few moments, before suggesting mildly, "Perhaps courier?"

I stared right back, wondering if he knew just how unaware he sounded. I was growing increasingly frustrated at Pavel's continual inability to give me clear, absolute information. This wasn't the first time he'd surprised me with a curveball, but it was definitely the most urgent – and expensive. He may have had great success with bigger clients who had more time and money to throw around, but he clearly wasn't well–suited to people like me. In hindsight, I would have checked out a few more recommendations before committing to an immigration specialist. I knew Michaela didn't think very much of Pavel, either. But unfortunately, I was already so far into this red–tape minefield that switching to someone else at such a late stage simply wasn't feasible. I'd just have to suck it up and sort it out, and give him my honest feedback later.

Fifty–one hours, far too many calls and emails, and several hundred euro later, I handed Pavel three copies of the slip of paper he'd asked for, in all its sparsely–written–bestamped glory which would have cost me almost nothing had I been given reasonable advance warning. He silently took the documents from me, skimmed each copy to make sure all was in order, and slipped them into the pile of paperwork that formed our three individual applications. No acknowledgement or apology whatsoever. He simply told me that he'd see me at the police station in the morning.

At 6.30am the following day, I overpaid the boorish taxi driver with great reluctance ("I say twenty euro, no five!") and hustled Tom and Pat out of the car. Only the driver had a seatbelt. Not that he had he used it, of course. He was too busy figuring out how to cheat me in his little bit of English. I had sat in the middle of the back seat, pinning the boys against it with outstretched arms and the strength that mild terror lends.

Even the grey grimness of the *Oddelenia cudzineckej polície* building in Petržalka, with its prison–like bars smothering every window and entrance of the former kindergarten, could not dim the pleasure the sweet warmth of that May breeze gave. Nor could it dampen my hope that we'd be finished quickly enough that the children wouldn't miss too much of the school day.

Pavel had suggested that we get there early to register our names before the station opened at 7.30am. He would come as quickly as he could to help translate. He had also arranged, for a fee, three placeholders to stand in line for me and the boys. It seemed to be a common practice, especially for people with children. Therefore, no one complained when I stepped into line where the teenage boys had been waiting with their cigarettes and beers since midnight on our behalf.

A queue of forty or fifty – likely more – very subdued–looking foreigners looped around the front of the building and out towards the pavement beyond. Perhaps fifteen of these were placeholders, eager to swap places with their clients as they arrived by foot or in taxis. Meanwhile, around a half–dozen sleeping bags were being rolled up and packed away as the sun rose higher and the line filled out.

There were only so many people that could be seen by the understaffed, overloaded alien police in one day. It was closed all day on Thursdays to process that week's paperwork, and for an hour on the other weekdays so that the harried officers could take a break. Securing a ticket could therefore be a game of chance and a test of endurance.

As I stood in line with the boys, keeping an eager eye out for Pavel, a burly man in his mid–twenties with a clipboard and an expression you didn't want to mess with, shuffled down the line and grunted at each person in Slovak, Russian, or broken English. When he reached the lady in front of me – a teacher from one of the international schools – she greeted him nervously in English.

"Name?"

She immediately gave it.

"You are not on list. Go to back of line."

"I'm sorry?"

"You. Are. Not. On. List. Back. Of. Line."

Still feeling pent–up crossness about the rude taxi driver, combined with nerves at finally handing in our applications, I debated whether to jump in and say something to support her. But the teacher didn't look like she was going to let some random person push her around, though. He wasn't wearing a uniform and clearly wasn't an official, although the police officers nearby ignored their exchange.

"Sorry, what's this list for? We were told to stand in line, so I'm standing in line."

Growing angry, the guy glared right into her eyes and insisted once again that she go to the back of the line. The eyes of everyone were upon her, though they were quick to look away when she silently appealed to them for back up. No one wanted to mess with this guy.

Uncertain what to do because of the kids, I looked around for Pavel to miraculously appear.

At that moment, a middle–aged Russian just ahead of us in a crisp white business shirt and slate trousers, and who looked every bit the equivalent of a mafioso, spat a few sharp words towards the aggressor. Unexpectedly, the clipboard guy immediately backed off, marched down the line, and began interrogating another unfortunate soul further along the queue.

The teacher had no idea if the Russian spoke English, but she thanked him anyway.

He snorted, amused at his own little bit of power. "They don't harass Igor. I'm here every day with clients. I was boxer in Russia. No list for Igor!"

I suddenly realised what this list actually was. It was not just any old list, but *The List*.

There were more than a few rumours about the infamous list in the online expat forums. With a limited number of police officers and an increasingly large number of applicants, it wasn't unheard of for people to wait here for eight hours or more – even longer if they'd camped out – only to be told to come back the next day. With the law stating that the alien police had ninety days to process the applications, and many non–EU applicants only having a ninety–day tourist stamp for the entire Schengen Zone, it wasn't rocket science to see how the odds were already stacked mightily against us. The list had come about as a grassroots attempt at fairness, a way to ensure that those who weren't seen that day, were first in line the next. Eventually, it had become an established under–the–radar arrangement, although by this time a semi–pro band of opportunists were doing their best to turn it into a profitable activity by taking advantage of the general confusion.

At 7.30am to the minute, a police officer in an unquestionably official uniform unlocked the door to the main entrance. With a burst of quiet energy, the queue sprang into action. Each person in turn gave their name to the officer and stepped through the entrance.

At that precise moment, a blonde–haired woman with a faux–playful bob and an attitude of complete confidence arrived on the scene in a cloud of powerful perfume. She calmly and with absolute entitlement marched to the top of the queue. She pulled a young moneyed student along in her wake, arm interlocked with hers. I had no idea how she did it, but with no hesitation the lawyer – for that's what she clearly was – and her client were ushered straight through ahead of the crowd. Quiet mutters of protest met this blatant display of queue jumping. But what could we do? Nothing more than shuffle into the waiting room to secure one of those highly–coveted tickets from the queue machine.

As I guided Pat and Tom into the waiting room, I observed a printed sign taped to the door inside a plastic cover, which read:

> *NOTICE*
> *We would like to inform you that The Department of Alien Police in Bratislava does not accept any "the list" with the names of foreigners whose are waiting for the ticket in front of the building of our Department. Every person has the right to get the ticket with number representing the exact time when the person came.*

Also, just within the door:

> *Udržujte poriadok!!!*
> *Keep clean!!!*

Standing amidst the throng and confusion with my three precious tickets in hand, I spotted Pavel finally pushing his way through the front door. He found himself and his briefcase a seat, secured me and the children seats nearby, and then began shuffling his papers into some sort of order.

I handed Tom and Pat their fully–charged tablets and some snacks, and very much hoped it would be enough to keep them occupied until this entire ordeal was over.

People began to be seen almost immediately. The digital board above the inner door flashed the first two ticket numbers, and the counter to go to. And there the numbers stayed numbingly put for fifteen to twenty minutes, until the next two suddenly flashed up on the screen.

The man beside me tapped his foot nervously in frustrated energy. Tap, tap, taptaptap; tap, tap, taptaptap. He caught my eye as I stole a sideways glance at his face.

"No, I'm not crazy," he grimaced. "It's my second time here this week."

"Oh. Are you renewing a permit, or registering, or…?" I asked hesitantly.

"Just updating my address. My address. I've been here a decade, yet I still have the misfortune of having to line up here. I was here yesterday with my wife and two kids. We walked in the door just after lunch, and it took them twenty minutes to get their cards sorted. Me? I waited four hours and didn't get seen, even though we came together."

"What happened?"

"The problem – or one of the problems, I should say – is those bloody machines. Almost anyone needing service from anyone in this building has to buy special stamps. They find this out when they finally get to the front of the queue and get called in to see an officer. So, they're sent back to find the *kolok* machine, wait in line, and eventually get to the machine. And of course, everything's in Slovak, and there's no one to help them and tell them which buttons to press and all that. So, while they're figuring this all out, and asking around for help from other people in the queue, and spending ten, twenty, thirty minutes sorting it out, everyone at the other building has to wait until that person returns. I sat there for four hours yesterday, and only about six people were processed. With three people still ahead of me, none of us got seen before they kicked us out and told us to come back today. I love Slovakia, I really do. Don't get me wrong. It's been ten years and I have a family here, after all. But I hate that we're treated like this," he griped, waving an arm around the room. "It's a bloody awful, awful mess. It's so deliberately useless – I mean deliberate at the political level. I can't say I blame the officers, not really. It's a mess above their heads. It must suck to work here."

Not in the mood for further discussion, he stared down at his shoes and continued with the incessant tapping.

If I wasn't nervous before, I certainly was now.

We waited several hours before our numbers were finally called.

Pavel handed over the paperwork to the officer at the designated counter. I stood beside him nervously, uncertain what to expect. The boys settled down on the floor at my feet, absorbed by their tablets.

"No." The officer barely bothered to look up from his coffee as he shoved the documents back to Pavel through the hole at the bottom of the counter window a few minutes later.

"No?"

"No. Not correct."

No further explanation was forthcoming.

His colleague to the left leaned towards Pavel with the air of a man who, for the sake of his reputation, didn't want to be seen as too helpful. "You need the official confirmation from *katastra*. Not from internet."

"OK."

"The children need to be on lease."

"OK."

"Come back with correct documents."

"OK."

Just like that, three OKs and four hours and fifty horrendous minutes later. I was aghast at having to go through this torture all over again. I was furious with Pavel, but did my best to remain cool in front of the officers.

"You've done this before, right?"

"*Áno*, I work with many big companies. Russia, Russian. Russian money."

I had no idea what that last bit meant, or suggested, but I was too fed up to stir the pot.

"None of my clients have children," he added as an aside.

I was livid. At my barely–polite insistence, Pavel ordered us a taxi. He shook my hand and promised he'd be in touch once he'd secured the official *katastra* document and spoken to Michaela again about the rental agreement.

My faith in him and this entire process was crashing down around me. I felt a strong urge to give up and save myself the hassle and expense before we fell in too deep. But, what was the alternative? Pavel's ever–changing interpretation of requirements for anyone who wasn't a single rich Russian client or corporation was equally matched by the frustrations and indignities that the authorities and list keepers appeared to revel in inflicting upon the foreigners brave enough to put themselves through this process.

Once the kids and I were in the taxi – a taxi with seatbelts this time – I texted Michaela a quick update. She replied almost instantly.

"WTF? That guy, what's he on? I did ask. That sucks. Absolutely useless!"

CHAPTER THIRTEEN

Once Michaela had double–checked the *Oddelenia cudzineckej polície* information herself to be sure, she quickly sorted out the updated rental agreement. I then contacted Dušan and Vilma to arrange for them to meet us to sign and notarise the pile of copies and declarations all over again.

With Pavel's legal advice continually concluding with, "It's possible we'll need it," or "Hopefully not," I wasn't taking any chances. As it was, Michaela was less than impressed with the job Pavel was doing, and was flabbergasted that he wasn't aware about the children needing to be on the lease. But he just had to get me and the boys through the application process as our existing power–of–attorney, and better hands could take over from there.

Of course, I hadn't told Michaela about the earlier revision to the rental agreement. Dušan and Vilma would therefore need to go through the farce of reprinting it all over again. I could only hope that another appointment would call Michaela conveniently away at just the right moment, without me having to make a separate appointment with the aunt and nephew. I just wanted it all over and done with as quickly as possible.

Vilma was away visiting another elderly relative in Austria, but Dušan was more than happy to handle the formalities in her absence. Conveniently, he held power–of–attorney status for his aunt given her frequent travels. Thankful for his willingness to make things as smooth as possible for me, I made a mental note to send them both some flowers and a bottle of wine when this was all over.

We met up outside the notary's office off Hurbanovo námestie. As it happened, Michaela did have a last–minute appointment to show an apartment ("It's almost always this way. I think I should rebrand myself as a 'Drop Everything and Run Specialist'"). She handed us the revised paperwork before hurrying off to her meeting on Kozia Street.

I waited in the grim lobby while Dušan slipped over to his aunt's apartment and her computer, just around the corner. He returned a few minutes later, printouts in hand.

We took the rickety lift up to the office. At the reception desk, the notary's no-nonsense assistant was thoroughly screening each visitor, prying out the most microscopic details of their requirements with nosey efficiency before shooing them to the austere waiting room with all the other walk-ins. Notaries ran roaring trades here in Slovakia.

Dušan sat next to me, patting a reassuring hand on my knee. I could see the blue veins bulging from his knuckles down to his wrist. Despite being in his fifties, his hands were otherwise perfectly smooth.

"The wait is the longest. The signatures are very fast. Payment even faster."

I nodded. I was already well-used to waiting around for officialdom to do its thing here. At least the kids were at school.

After a twenty-one-minute wait, we were finally called into the office. Behind the room-dominating desk of a sombre shade, a middle-aged lady with a stern expression and dull greying hair peered sharply at us over the top of her glasses.

"*Prosím?*"

Dušan explained in Slovak the reason for our visit, and produced the updated copies of the rental agreement.

The notary scrutinised each page carefully, nodded slowly, and called in her assistant. The assistant peered over her boss's shoulder as the last page of each copy was lined up ready for our signatures and the official stamp. Suddenly, she put her bulbous lips up close to the other woman's ear and whispered in an urgent tone. The notary tipped her head to one side, thought for a moment, then indicated her agreement. She looked up and calmly addressed Dušan in Slovak.

Whatever it was she said immediately precipitated a furious back-and-forth between the assistant and Dušan, with the latter becoming increasingly irate as his explanations were rejected summarily by both. He stood up, his chair nearly falling backwards as he muttered angrily at the notary and her assistant. Neither were in the least bit fazed by his sudden aggression.

The assistant came around to the front of the desk, and silently pointed at the door. Dušan and I were then abruptly escorted out of the office with our paperwork.

Once we were safely in the lift, Dušan exploded. "These women, they think they are kings."

"What's the problem?" I asked cautiously. I was astonished at his venom.

"Ah well, they say my power–of–attorney for my aunt should be original, not notary copy. I used this same copy last week at their office, and it was OK, no one says nothing. The original and copy are made by them! That other woman, not even a notary. What do they care? Last week was last week, they say. This week, different rules. Stupid. So, we must find another notary."

I remembered seeing one in the Tatra Centrum a few days earlier, when I had been there to do some shopping. Dušan nodded. It was a four–minute walk, if that.

Within ten minutes we had arrived at the notary's office, had our paperwork reviewed and notarised, paid the fee, and stepped back into the lift.

"I will use this notary in future," Dušan declared as we descended to the ground floor in the modern lift. "No looking for problems, just business. This is how it should be."

"How much was the notary?" I asked. He had paid the fee before I could step forward and pay it myself, and I wasn't yet familiar with the sound of numbers in Slovak. "I'll pay the fee, of course. I really appreciate the time you've taken to sort this out. I'm just really sorry it's been so frustrating."

"No, it is my pleasure. The time and amount are very little. Perhaps you can buy some wine sometime to make it smooth, yes? We will meet together so you can tell me your story."

"Um, sure. Let me know when Vilma is back, and we can make arrangements."

"Unfortunately, my aunt will go away for some time. Our relative is not well."

"I'm so sorry to hear that."

"Thank you. She is old; she has not been very well for many months."

Dušan waved me ahead of him out the lift with one hand, the other clutching his satchel. His hand slid against my thigh as he stepped back in line beside me. His shiny cheeks immediately flushed scarlet, and he looked away.

I wrote it off as accidental, and let it go. I wasn't a fan of his touchy–feely habits though, no matter how friendly he was. If it kept happening, I'd have to have a word with him to explain our obvious cultural differences when it came to physical space. In the meantime, I'd be sure to keep a little more distance between us in future.

"Hmmm, that's definitely a bit creepy," Michaela decided as she sipped on her *espresso lungo*. We had been getting along quite well, so I was delighted when she got in touch to suggest coffee and cake at Café Dobre & Dobre on Nedbalova Street, just behind the old market. I appreciated her directness and sense of humour, not to mention the opportunity to discuss things other than Lego, cars, and bodily functions with someone close to my own age.

"That's what I thought. I told Andy last night, and he said a lot of his male friends here were super friendly with women. But that was ten years ago, and they were all in their twenties and thirties. And probably drunk half the time. So, I don't know."

"No Slovak guy I know would be that consistently friendly unless he's a creep, and I've lived in Bratislava all my life."

"Dušan mentioned they're from the east of Slovakia."

"Maybe that makes a difference. They're practically a separate people out there. Well, my advice would be to just keep your distance so he doesn't get the wrong idea. I think he's single, right? So, you never know, maybe he's just looking for a wife to help run the business and make him breakfast."

"Yeah, no thank you. I'm not jumping onto that wagon again any time soon."

As ever, Michaela had an appointment afterwards. When we were done, we asked for the bill and paid for our orders.

While I waited for her to return from the bathroom, I quickly checked my phone for any client messages.

A notification from Józef sat on the screen.

"Hiya! I have a conference coming up in Bratislava. If you're around, we can go for a drink afterwards." He then sent a follow-up message with the proposed date.

My reaction was a thunderbolt of nostalgic sentimentality, followed by a slap of nerves at the idea of seeing him again, and so soon. I'd almost forgotten about him these past few weeks, so distracted had I been by everything going on.

I read his short message over and over, sweaty palms and the jitters increasing with every re-reading.

He couldn't know this, of course. I was determined to play it cool. Well, a little cool.

I typed out a reply while I waited for Michaela, re-read it, and edited it a couple more times. 'Great! I think I'm around then. Drop me a line closer to the time, and we'll make arrangements."

There. Done. Sent.

CHAPTER FOURTEEN

Our second visit to the alien police was just as tedious, although marginally less stressful. Why this couldn't be done via an online appointment system was beyond me.

There was no 'list' today, at least. A wave of recent media attention had temporarily put a halt to the practice until the latest furore died down. It was still a heaving, impatient, unwilling crush, made worse by the lack of English or any other of the more common languages to give people an idea as to what they were actually supposed to do. Almost all of the most important instructions were in Slovak, as were the queue and *kolok* machines, both of which were interacted with almost exclusively by non–Slovak speakers. The International Organization for Migration had been tolerated to put up some posters in English about Slovak language courses, or on how to return to one's own country. Other than that, everything was in Slovak. As the alien police were not encouraged to speak English, this meant that every applicant needed to bring an interpreter with them, or attempt to do the interview through gestures and grunts.

More at ease by knowing what to expect this time at least, my attitude was one of moderate whatever–ness. The kids were again distracted with snacks and their tablets. They didn't seem to mind being back here again, for all the boredom and long wait. It just gained them extra tablet time that they normally wouldn't have. Win–win.

Pavel had arranged with me to call him when the displayed number reached five before my own ticket, rather than having him wait there the entire time. This was perfectly fine with me.

The wait for an officer – any officer – was excruciating. But there was no point in complaining: it had to be done. It was, I had to admit, a rather fascinating process to be a part of, in spite of the frustration. One day in the future, the post–communist chaos of the alien police would be modernised and streamlined, surely.

While we waited, the mini–parodies going on in the waiting room kept me more than entertained, if not occasionally furious. For over forty minutes, two technicians had been working on the ticket dispenser, which had broken down within twenty minutes of the station opening for business. From all their apathetic standing around and half–hearted phone calls, it was easy to see that they had absolutely no idea what was wrong with it. Unfortunately, without a ticket from the machine as proof of when you arrived, applications could not be processed, and the individual would simply have to return another day. The machine being out of order was neither here nor there to the harried officers. They had a job to do, and that was that.

I watched with increasing pity the frustration and anger of the dozen or so people waiting on foot for the machine to be fixed. The technicians, as if unaware of the machine's importance and not speaking anything other than Slovak, slackened and chatted as they waited for a more experienced colleague to arrive.

In the meantime, a university student was making urgent rounds of the waiting room, her drop earrings clicking as she leaned in to repeat her question to one person after another. The interpreter who was supposed to come with her had cancelled at the last moment, leaving her desperately trying to find someone else to help. She had already been to the station twice with additional paperwork, so her time and patience were running out. She eventually managed to negotiate the services of a translator who had come with another client. They shook hands, the fee was paid, and the student took a relieved seat to wait her turn.

After a couple more hours, our number crept tantalisingly closer. I sent Pavel a quick text, telling him to head to Petržalka.

He arrived just as our number flashed up on the screen. Bristling with importance, he accompanied me and the boys through the waiting room door and up to our assigned counter, his expression arranged into one of comical obsequiousness.

Our case was handled that day by a young officer with an army regulation–style haircut, not long assigned to Bratislava from a very rural location. With a high turnover at the alien police, junior officers who would not otherwise have dreamt of the bright lights of Bratislava so early in their careers, were transferred to the alien department in the hopes of future reassignment elsewhere if they played their cards right.

The officer was perfectly nice, if incredibly slow and methodical. He hadn't been in the job very long, and took every little detail of it absolutely seriously. This time, however, we came very well–prepared. Try as the officer might to find something, anything, amiss with our applications to please his superiors with his attention to detail, nothing could be found. After ninety minutes, the three applications were fully entered into his computer. Tom, Pat, and I had our photos taken by one of his colleagues for our ID cards, and then we were finally free to go. I felt exhilarated.

Pavel stood with us almost–silently as we waited for our taxi to arrive. We then shook hands, with Pavel promising to get in touch when he received the notification that our permits were ready to be picked up.

Now, the long wait began. We had already been in Bratislava for five weeks by this point. I was pinning my hopes on an unlikely miracle that somehow the cards would arrive in the next seven weeks, before our twelve–week visa–free stamps expired. Until then, I would do my very best not to worry about it.

I dropped the children off at school, and took the taxi the rest of the way home. I hoped to get a bit of work done in the few hours left in the school day, before it was time to head out and collect the boys.

In the courtyard, Dušan was busy discussing a maintenance project with a worker. One arm rested on the light brown leather satchel lying across his shoulder as he went over some instructions with the contractor.

As soon as he spotted me, Dušan strode over to say hello.

"Was it a success?" he enquired, beaming hopefully.

"Yes, it's all submitted now. I think everything went smoothly. Now, we just have to wait and see. Thank you again for everything."

He shook his head. "It was my pleasure." He then stared down at my neck, puzzled. "Are you not cold? The weather, it is not so nice today."

Actually, I felt perfectly warm. I was wearing a black dress, thick black tights, and a V–neck vermilion jumper. It was a little cool, but definitely not what I'd consider cold.

"It's OK, I'm used to it. It's colder in Canada at this time of year, anyway," I smiled politely.

Before I could react, Dušan leaned forward and pressed the left side of his warm, oily face down against the exposed area of my upper chest, with a drawn–out "Ah!". His satchel slid forward as he did so, smacking into my side with a firm thud.

I stepped back in disbelief at what he'd just done. The young worker standing beside Dušan merely smirked and looked away.

"I wanted to see if you're cold. I can feel it that you are. Please, you must go and put on something warm," Dušan instructed.

I simply stared up at him, too astonished for displeasure. Who was he to touch me, to tell me how to dress? If this is how older men behaved here, it was definitely not going to be a case of 'when in Rome'.

I hurried up the stairs to my apartment without another word, and locked the door very firmly behind me.

CHAPTER FIFTEEN

Coffee with Ján had become a very enjoyable regularity. We'd met up several times over the past few weeks, and I'd come to appreciate his understated sense of humour. He was relaxed and open, interested and interesting, complex yet not complicated, and never attempted to flirt. In other words, he was very refreshing.

As Ján wasn't much of a morning person, we usually met up around lunch–time, when he was much more alert and much less likely to switch to German or Slovak when he thought he was speaking English.

Our discussions were wonderfully stimulating and varied. While the state of American politics at that time always gave us plenty to talk about, our conversations ranged broadly from history, cultural affairs, music, news, and books to technology and cryptocurrencies. And, of course, food. We were both 'foodies', despite his teasing raised eyebrow at a non–meat eater calling herself such.

Thanks to him, I was slowly being introduced to some of the best places to eat in Bratislava. Ironically, he almost never ate when we met up, aside from the occasional slice of cake, as he would usually have a late breakfast before heading into town. Sometimes I ate, but mostly I'd have a latte or two while he slowly sipped away on his single espresso.

On this particular day, we met up at Urban Space on Námestie SNP, with its trendy ripped sofas and eclectic range of books in Slovak and English. Naturally, it was popular with the hipster crowd. Its tables and chairs were dotted with university students discussing projects and flirting over their drinks, twenty–

somethings doing business with their open jackets without ties, and individual souls quietly reading books while savouring their over–sized cappuccinos.

Ján had already told me he wasn't a fan of galleries or museums, but somehow we got talking about Bratislava's history, and from there we moved on to socialist architecture.

"Well, I can't say I'm a fan, even to be polite," I declared. "In my mind, I associate it with minimalist architecture and brutalism, and I associate both with the destruction of a lot of classical architecture back in the 60s. When I lived in Dublin, there was a whole row of Georgian buildings, all in perfectly good condition from what I understand, knocked down by the Electricity Supply Board to make way for their headquarters. Until then, it was the longest stretch of Georgian houses in the world. I'm talking about a truly ugly, characterless building they thought was all the rage in 60s or 70s minimalism. Can you imagine? Ugh. It was absolutely awful, and no one I know had anything good to say about it. Not surprisingly, they knocked it down not so long ago. It was just a horrible, brown, boring eyesore. The only thing I'd say weakly in its favour was that it was a very even and clean design. Functional."

"But maybe that's the point. It was probably meant to be clean and functional. Socialist architecture and minimalist architecture are something similar, I think. For us, it came at a time of communism and a time of functional necessity. There's something attractive in the purpose of these designs; maybe not the obvious beauty you think is important, but still very nice. Like the Slovensky Rozhlas building, or the UFO bridge. The bridge has no pillars, and this makes it different. Functional, minimalist, clean, different. I like this style. These are my thoughts, anyway."

"I just think the irony is that, although I guess they wanted to avoid being associated with a particular period of time – to be timeless, if you will – such designs actually created a new period of time in architecture. As we've moved away from the harshness of this approach – yes, I'd say harshness – minimalism, whether it's the Bauhaus–inspired minimalism or communist–influenced brutalism – it's unavoidably identifiable with a certain period of the twentieth century. I mean that we can look at it and say, ah yes, that belongs to the 60s or whatever. I could be wrong, of course."

Ján offered a diplomatic smile, and the conversation moved on to another topic.

Although I wouldn't have admitted it at the time, our discussion had left me with a strong interest in learning more about some of these buildings in Bratislava that I had previously thought so unappealing. Not that I was willing to budge on my long–held opinion just yet. But I quietly decided to check out these more obvious examples through the filter of his opinion before jumping back up on my little soap box.

My daily routine during the week almost inevitably involved coffee.

It invariably began by purchasing a *syrové rožok* – a cheesy breadstick – from the Naglreiter bakery on Obchodná, and stopping by Pán Králiček on my way to or from dropping Tom and Pat off at school.

On this particular day, I was the only person in the queue for once. Oskar was on shift, and was more than happy to stop and chat while things were quiet.

He was tremendously sweet that morning. It was Children's Day in Slovakia, and the boys were extremely excited about the events planned at school that day. They had grown fond of Oskar over the past few weeks, and enjoyed giggling and chatting with him while he prepared my coffee. He handled their high–pitched exclamations with patient enthusiasm, and occasionally tried to persuade me to let them share a free hot chocolate, despite my misgivings about them making a mess of their school clothes.

On the day in question, he admitted he'd got there twenty minutes early to be sure of catching us. To the boys' delight he presented them with an espresso cup of strawberries and a matching quantity of melted chocolate to dip the fruit into.

"Come on, they have one day a year," he smiled at me. He then stared down at the excited boys. "Now, your mother needs her coffee. Sit over there, laddies," he told them, gesturing to a seat next to the ice box. "Don't make a mess."

I breathed in the scent of freshly–ground coffee beans as Oskar prepared my latte. I was an enthusiast for their coffee: it was a little chocolatey, and not at all bitter. It was so smooth that I had even begun to wean myself off the touch of sugar I'd been in the habit of adding to it.

But I had to admit that a large part of my dedication to Pán Králiček, rather than their nearby rival, were the lively chats I had with Oskar and Eva and some of the other servers. Tom and Pat knew each of them by name, and were sure to be greeted cheerfully whenever we stopped by. Oskar and Eva were their clear favourites, however.

Oskar's English was excellent, and he was a good conversationalist.

"So, is there really a Pán Králiček?" I asked.

"Yes, he's real. He's the owner."

"Is he ever out here serving coffee?" I wondered, trying to guess which one he could be.

"Oh god no," Oskar smirked. "We don't let him serve. He's better at managing."

At that moment, the homeless man that I'd seen here before slowly approached us, dragging his suitcase and bags with practised effort.

Oskar introduced us as he poured out the milk. "Miloš speaks English, you know."

"Really?"

"Yes, I learned in middle school, many many many years ago. English was not common. We normally learned German. I didn't use English for long time, especially during communism time. But now so many tourists are here. I speak it often. But perhaps, not very well."

"You speak beautifully."

"Thank you, thank you," Miloš beamed. "I have seen you here many times before with your children, I think."

"You've *heard* my children many times before, I'm sure," I replied. "I'm still working on getting them to lower their little voices in public."

"It's true, they have personality," Oskar winked.

"That's a polite way to put it," I grinned back.

As more customers came up and Oskar became distracted, I chatted with Miloš for a few minutes longer while the boys messily finished their strawberries and chocolate. It was hard to determine exactly how old he was. I figured somewhere in his mid–sixties, although his weather–worn complexion likely added a few more years. At one point, he mentioned accommodation and needing to be out during the day, so I guessed that he lived in an overnight emergency shelter.

The boys finally finished their treat. Oskar handed them a cloth to wipe themselves down with.

I smiled at Miloš. "I have to go now, unfortunately. The boys should be at school soon."

"Maybe I'll talk to you again sometime?" he asked.

"Of course. It's been very interesting chatting with you. I see you around town a lot."

"Even when he's feeling sick or the weather is not so good, Miloš follows the same schedule," Oskar grinned, listening in. "It's easy to predict when and where to find him. He's here in the mornings until nine o'clock, then he takes a long walk. You'll find him in Naglreiter having a snack between three and four, and then on Hviezdoslavovo námestie from four until six–thirty. Miloš likes to walk a lot. He knows Bratislava well."

"I must get some tips from you some time, then," I told him. "Well, it's been lovely chatting to you. Enjoy the rest of your day."

Oskar smiled and waved as the boys squealed out their thanks and good–byes. They were looking forward to telling the kids at school about their surprise second breakfast.

CHAPTER SIXTEEN

Andy's flight from Montréal was due in at 10.30am. The boys and I got the 8.30am bus from Most SNP for the forty–five minute journey to the airport in Vienna.

The Austrian police had been stepping up their random border checks lately. I'd been nervous about travelling without Slovak temporary residency permits, even though we had valid passports. To my relief, our bus was not selected this time.

At the airport, we tucked into a late breakfast while we waited for the flight to arrive. As soon as Andy's plane had landed, we finished up our meals, paid the bill, and sidled into good viewing spots at the railing outside the glass doors where arriving passengers flowed through.

The Schwechat airport authorities were generally very efficient, and I knew it wouldn't be long before Andy appeared. Sure enough, arrivals from Canada soon began making their way through the doors. Wriggling like over–excited puppies, Tom and Pat raced into their father's arms as soon as he came through.

"It's funny, you look bigger somehow," I commented as I kissed him on the cheek. "I guess it's all those video calls staring at a smaller version of you."

"Maybe. Listen, I need a cigarette. Like, badly. I haven't had one since Montreal."

I remembered passing a smoke–filled bar a little along the hall from where we'd eaten breakfast, and pointed it out to him. Andy hurried along to get his nicotine hit while the kids delighted in an unexpected second apple juice while playing with a toy their father had given them.

We'd previously made plans to spend the day in Vienna before catching a late afternoon bus back to Bratislava. It was a Saturday, so the kids were off school and we had the entire day ahead of us to enjoy the city.

I adored Vienna. I'd first fallen in love with it after reading *Diaries, 1898– 1902: Alma Mahler–Werfel* when I was nineteen; a similar age to Alma in the diaries. She was a world away from me in upbringing, but the liveliness of her writing about the city and its culture, and the artistic and musical circles her family moved in, fostered my lifelong fascination for *fin de siècle* Vienna. I'd travelled there several times over the years, sometimes tracing Alma's footsteps, but mostly soaking in the culture and seeking out the works of and connections to Gustav Klimt, Carl Moll, Alexander von Zemlinsky, Max Burckhard and the other Secessionist artists, and, of course, Gustav Mahler. Even though he'd lived a good century before Alma, one of my favourite possessions was a little white bust of Mozart; mass–produced for tourists, of course, but a decent enough reproduction of one of my music heroes.

That particular day in Vienna, however, was devoted almost entirely to entertaining the boys. And eating, of course. Vienna was, after all, famous for its sweet delights. I had a very soft spot for *Mozartkugeln*, those delicious dark chocolate–covered balls of pistachio marzipan and nougat sold all over Austria.

When Andy had finished his cigarette, the four of us jumped onto an express train into town.

We got off at Karlsplatz and walked directly to the city centre in the mid– morning sunshine, dropping Andy's bag off at a luggage storage facility along the way. We then wandered up Kärntner Strasse, in between the tourists taking selfies and waiters puffing on a quick cigarette between customers and the hawkers selling tattered magazines and souvenirs to unsuspecting tourists.

Eventually, we found a café we could all agree upon through a vote of noses pressed eagerly against the window. Andy and I ushered the boys inside the brightly–lit Sluka Conditorei, ogling the cakes and pastries as we made our way to an empty table. Finally, with much mind–changing about what to have, the waiter patiently took our orders. He was back just as quickly with hot chocolate for the boys, a glossy golden *Klimt Torte* and a latte for me, and an *Apfelstrudel* and *Franziskaner* coffee for Andy.

"Pure Vienna," I sighed, licking the foam around the inner rim of my cup.

We spent the rest of the afternoon in the bustling Museumsquartier; the kids and Andy at the children's museum, me at the Secession. After several months of solo parenting, I was ecstatic at the opportunity to hang out by myself in Vienna for a while.

As the late afternoon sky began to drop hints of eve, we caught the bus to Bratislava. Back at Most SNP, we collected Andy's bulging wheeled suitcase from the hold, and took a slightly–circuitous route to my apartment through the centre of the old town. Andy was curious to see if anything had changed much since he was last there.

At that time of day, the streets were buzzing with tourists and early diners searching for a place to eat or grab a drink. The air was grill– and hookah–scented from the wide–open doors of restaurants and cafés.

As we walked through the cobbled streets, I couldn't help but sneak curious peeks at Andy's face. I watched his eyebrows go up or a smile touch his lips as certain memories came back to him.

Then, after dropping Andy's suitcase off, the four of us headed to nearby Bruno's for some pizza. For an Italian restaurant literally just around the corner from the massive Crowne Plaza Hotel, somehow it seemed to remain a hidden gem, in part thanks to its discrete signage. I wasn't complaining – we almost always managed to get a table without a reservation.

And so we ate, and drank, and paid the bill. Andy was beginning to feel the effects of jet lag, and the boys were worn out from their busy day, so none of them protested about having an early night. I took advantage of the peace to catch up on some work while the three of them tumbled into their respective beds.

Aside from Andy's loud and irregular snores, surreal after so many weeks, no interruption punctured the peace of my otherwise silent evening.

Andy's few weeks in Slovakia rolled by at a steady enough pace. In many ways, our former domestic routine – placid and uneventful – continued much as before. Our conversations were easy and unforced; we both still enjoyed long, often heated discussions about the current state of American politics. He joined in the school runs and shopping trips, and we both did our work from the kitchen table with lap–tops and coffee mugs practically back–to–back. In the evenings we worked or watched documentaries, aside from the nights when he would slip out to meet one of his old friends, or have a smoke and a drink at Next Apache, which was just around the corner from my place. It was all very quiet and familiar. This was no bad thing in the general scheme of things, I suppose, but it was a powerful reminder of how closeted I'd felt by my former life. It wasn't Andy's fault. As friends we got along very well; as partners our interests and energy levels were simply no longer compatible. I had little doubt he felt exactly the same about me.

With Andy on hand to share the parenting, I delighted in the freedom of being able to go out at night if I wanted to. And I did. Michaela and I took advantage of the very first opportunity to meet up at Café Verne on Hviezdoslavovo námestie – or Unpronounceable Square as I preferred to call it.

According to Ján, the square was named after one of his ancestors. No matter how many times they individually tried to teach me how to pronounce it ("Huh – vyez – do – slah – vo – vo"), I could never quite get my tongue around it.

I'd already eaten dinner, but Michaela was practically starving. She called over the waiter for a menu, and perused it intently before settling on a cheese dish. After a twenty–minute wait because of the Friday night crowd, the server finally brought her dinner to our table. It smelled delicious.

"God, I love the food in Bratislava," I exclaimed. "I just love the different scents as you walk down the streets. The warm pastries, hot chocolate, garlic, pretzels, schnitzel, and oh, the coffee…"

"… the body odour, the drains," Michaela added helpfully.

I laughed.

"So, how's it going with Andy?" Michaela wanted to know as she tucked into her meal.

"It's all good. We're just continuing on pretty much as we used to."

"In *every* respect?" Michaela grinned.

"No comment," I smiled, sipping my wine. "He left Bratislava when his girlfriend of the time broke up with him, so I thought it might be tough for him. But he seems happier than not to be back. He's been out a few times with old friends, checking out the places they used to hang out in. And it's great to have an extra pair of hands with the kids."

"I bet. I don't know how you do it on your own. And what's happening with the police?"

I filled her in on Pavel's latest bout of uselessness regarding an update on our applications.

"Well, no can accuse him of doing his job," Michaela declared. "If it gets too much, just let me know. I'll get you the contact info for that lawyer I was telling you about, the one who does it for George and his team. He's good. Very good."

"I might have to take you up on that if things get any worse," I promised. "It's almost impossible to get a clear update out of him. I don't mind if there's no update, but don't tell me you're going to keep me regularly updated if you do no such thing, and then ignore my messages. I feel like he's got my money now, so he doesn't really care what comes next."

"And Dušan, has he been creepy lately?"

"He and Vilma are away with his parents right now. Turkey, I think they said. Just as well. Andy was going to speak to him if he saw him."

We stayed for another couple of hours, chatting away over a few glasses of wine. Then Michaela walked me back to my apartment in the crisp evening air before heading through the presidential palace underpass to catch her bus. We hugged goodbye, promising to definitely have another girls' night out again soon.

A few days before Andy's visit was to come to an end, we sat in the living room after the boys had gone to bed, sipping on a drink.

"You seem to be having a great time back here," I commented.

Andy nodded. "I guess I'd forgotten what it's like. I'm surprised by all the changes. There're definitely more restaurants and malls than when I was here. Everything seems brighter, more... European? Slovakia had just joined the EU when I left. I guess they've tapped into all that EU money to improve the infrastructure. I see lots of big corporate and residential blocks have gone up, too. In my time, there was nothing where Eurovea is. Now, it's a massive shopping mall, the Sheraton, the national theatre, restaurants along the boardwalk there, and that new development just getting started opposite."

"Doesn't it make you want to consider coming back?"

"Hmmm, maybe one day."

"One day? Not a little sooner than 'one day'?"

"My business is on Prince Edward Island. I can't just leave it."

"You can do anything you want to. Didn't I?"

"You're different. I'm not like you. I never felt the urge to come back here like you did. Not really."

"You used to tell me something different. I held on to that for years, you know, the fact you said you'd move back over within a year or two after we left Germany, as soon as we got some money together."

"Yes, but we didn't have any money until my dad gave us some for the house, did we?"

I had consumed a couple of glasses of wine by then. I decided to be bold, to speak how I really felt.

"I'm sorry to say it, but I resented you for that for a long time. While I was working hard, doing my best to get money in for us, you were always so reactive and never followed up on leads unless pushed. I never understood that. I'm a big reason your business got started, a big reason for us not sinking a long, long time ago. I think you forget that."

"I don't forget that. But I just don't want to hear it over and over again, whenever you get mad at me for the way I do things. I'm running the business entirely on my own now, with no one pushing me. Sure, I admit, maybe I'd be doing a lot better if I wasn't so lazy, but I'm doing it. I'm doing it the way I want to do it. It's nothing to do with you anymore."

"Us not being there, family life not distracting you, must help." I countered.

Andy sighed. "What do you want me to say to that?"

We were silent for a few moments, teetering on the brink of escalation. But the wine had got to me, and I simply couldn't help myself.

"I don't think you ever loved me. I'm not stupid."

"I did love you. But this was your decision, remember, not mine. I had to move on, and so I moved on."

"Don't you miss the boys and the life we had?"

"Of course. I miss the boys and the life and all that. But you decided this."

"You mean, you're enjoying the bachelor life too much," I retorted. "No one to push you or remind you to do everything, no kids underfoot, you can eat out whenever you want, play computer games all night, smoke your pot and no one cares."

"That's not entirely true," Andy rebutted. "I won't lie, there's a lot of truth in that, but it's not the whole story. I work hard, too. Well, I work. I'm not like you like that – our definition of 'work hard' is different. But this was your choice, remember. You can't blame me for what I do with my own life. You can't have it both ways."

"I just kind of hoped you'd end us missing us, missing me, and finally pull your finger out and do something about it. Clearly, I was wrong."

"I do miss it all. But I'm just not ready to think about the future. Sorry."

"You can't expect me to wait in limbo, with you maybe yes–ing and maybe no–ing about the future."

"Well, don't then. What can I tell you? I don't know. Maybe in four or five years, I'll consider moving over here for the kids, not you."

I felt the cold fingers of shock sink into me.

"Oh my god. How is that supposed to make me feel? That I made the decision to leave precisely because you backtracked on wanting to move back here, and now you're telling me it's something you'd consider in the future but – and here's the kicker – not for me! You'd come here and do everything I wanted you to do and be, but just without me being part of it!"

"I'm sorry, I don't mean it like that."

"What else could you mean by that?"

Andy was not one for strong emotion, nor for dealing with angry women. He took advantage of the moment to get up and slip outside to calm himself with some pot. It was a habit I had no liking for, but it usually made it easier to communicate with him about difficult issues. So, I kept my mouth shut and let him go.

When Andy came back a few minutes later with a nervous attempt at a grin on his face, I decided to just let it go. He was leaving in three days. He knew how I felt. There was nothing I could do to influence him, and everything I could do to alienate. He'd probably be back again in a couple of months, closer to the time when a decision could be made about going ahead with the divorce.

CHAPTER SEVENTEEN

Once Andy had returned to Canada, the boys and I snapped back into our usual routine very quickly.

The boys now attended an excellent international kindergarten on Gajova Street. I'd put their names down on the waiting list back in Canada, and had long forgotten about it. I received a call in mid–June to say they finally had spaces available, so I transferred the children there as soon as the school year ended two weeks later. It was a much bigger school than the Montessori, and a lot easier for me to get to. They also offered a year–round programme, which was a huge attraction given my busy freelance work. Now we could walk or take their scooters to school in less than twenty minutes, rather than the previous forty–five minute walk–bus–bus–walk routine.

It also meant that we passed directly by Pán Králiček on the way. My order was so well–known by now that the servers generally got my latte going as soon as they spotted me or heard the boys coming down the street. It was a delightful little courtesy; it made me feel very much at home.

Around this time, I finally gave in to Tom's pleadings for a violin. The boys were fascinated by the street musicians who played classical and folk music by the underpass entrance opposite Café Dias. In particular, they loved watching the young violinist – a cheerful, dark–skinned youth in his early twenties – and dancing along to the music.

Many years before, I'd worked as a freelance writer for a classical music magazine for a couple of years. So, I was secretly delighted at Tom's sudden interest in the violin. He was young enough to learn and he was certainly eager. I figured there could be little harm in letting him try.

From our regular chats, I knew that Ján had an interest in music. He agreed immediately when I asked if he'd be willing to translate for me at the instrument shop.

We met up on a bright July afternoon while the kids were at school, and walked to Dowina on Medená Street. With Ján's help, the assistant got a good understanding of what I needed, and gave me a choice between two beginner violins for children. On a crazy impulse, I got myself a violin, too. Surely it wouldn't be too hard to remember the basics I'd learned during those Saturday morning classes in Dublin all those years ago, right?

Ján didn't stop there with his help. He tapped into his connections and found us a private teacher through a friend–of–a–friend; a university student who was trained in violin and music theory. She was bubbly and enthusiastic, but ultimately nervous about her English, and gave up the lessons after the first couple of meetings.

Hearing the news, Ján promised to do his best to help find a replacement. His quiet thoughtfulness was really very endearing. There was absolutely nothing in it for him except to be supportive: no agenda, no expectations of any kind. He'd been exactly the same from the moment we first met again. I occasionally tried to pay for his coffee or surreptitiously round up my share of our restaurant bills to quietly express my thanks, but he almost never let me get away with that. I was grateful for his genuine soul in this still–unfamiliar city.

Speaking of July: before I knew it, Józef was due in town.

On the day of his arrival, I did my best not to think too much about it. But who was I kidding? I was a bundle of nerves as I counted down the hours and minutes and then the seconds to when he was likely to finish his conference, exchange niceties with the other participants, get his jacket and his briefcase together, walk the short distance back to his hotel, catch up on his work emails, freshen himself up, and stop by my place for dinner.

The plan had originally been to meet at a restaurant, but I hadn't been able to find an English–speaking babysitter who was available that particular night. Tom and Pat were already in bed when Józef rang my doorbell, exhausted by a fantastically–timed mini–Olympics event at their new school that day.

I'd forgotten how tall he was as he stood in the doorway, with lean muscular legs like a basketball player. The perception of his height was familiarly enhanced by that give–nothing–away expression with which he had always faced the world.

I kissed him on the cheek; he accepted it.

Smiling, Józef closed the door behind him. He handed me a bottle of wine, took off his jacket, and thanked me for the invitation.

After not having seen him in so long, those first few moments felt tremendously awkward. If Józef felt this too, he didn't show it.

"So. It's good to see you," he said, breaking the silence as we sat down to eat.

"Likewise. It's been so long!"

"Can I just say, you look even better now than you did all those years ago?"

I smiled to myself at his habitual compliments for the ladies.

"Thank you. You look pretty good yourself."

"You've put on a couple of kilos, but you've had kids, that's OK. It happens. I prefer women not to be too skinny. You look great."

I wasn't sure whether to be mildly offended or amused by the back–handed compliment. But as I generally preferred to find the ridiculous in everything, I just laughed.

"You need to loosen up and express yourself. Let me get you a drink!"

His eyes twinkled with amusement as he raised an eyebrow at me.

Dinner was soon over, and so we moved to the sofa to continue our chat. Józef brought the wine bottle with him, topping me up and then himself. We clinked glasses, staring straight into each other's eyes as was the European custom.

"How's your mother?" I enquired, cutting through yet another silence.

"She's good, as always. She sends you her greetings. I've got a small gift from her for you in my jacket. Remind me to give it to you before I go. She's happy we get to meet again."

"Thank you. Please send her my greetings in return."

"I will, thank you."

"And…?" I needed more wine.

"And what?"

"Your wife. So, tell me in person, not just in writing. What happened?"

"Where do I start? It's a long story."

"OK. Let's start with, do you love her?"

"Straight to the point with wine, I see. Well, we have a kid," was his cryptic reply. "Actually, to be honest, I didn't see this coming – I thought everything was OK and she never said anything, so I was… surprised, to say the least. In the spring she was talking about having another kid, and two months later she moved out with our son."

"What were her reasons? Did she ever tell you?"

"I got a long email. Basically, she was unhappy that I bought a car without her approval. We already had a family car, and I wanted one for me. I could afford it. She didn't like that idea. Also, the brand was wrong. She likes designer labels, big names. It wasn't good enough. Lots of other complaints. Anyway, I didn't read the whole letter. Her parents, they're rich, so they bought her an apartment. They don't like me that much."

"Why not?"

"I don't know. The age gap. High expectations."

"You? Mr. University Lecturer, successful business man, would–be politician? Why aren't you good enough for them?"

He grinned at the description. "You'd have to ask them."

I raised my eyebrows, perplexed. "And so, that's all she had to complain about? Seems strange that she'd leave you over a car. Maybe you're being too hard on yourself."

"Like I said, it was a long message. Long, and rather repetitive. There were other issues, but I didn't read it all. Anyway, enough of my sad love stories. What about you and your husband?"

"Well, we're doing OK. I mean, of course, we're still separated and all, but we're really nailing the amicable thing. He gets my reasons for doing what I did. He's supportive. I couldn't be luckier in that respect, to be honest."

"Will you get back together?"

"No, I don't think so."

"Why not?"

"We talked about it when he was here. Neither of us really wants to. He seems pretty happy doing the bachelor thing. He splashed out on virtual reality stuff, he bought a new computer, he's got a new car – a single guy car. He seems to be gleefully living up the single life without wife and kids. I don't think he'd be in a hurry to give that all up again. Anyway, as you know, our ideal life paths are no longer compatible. I can't do that anymore. The kids are happy, they love their school, they speak to him every day on Skype. We've made it as normal and adventure–like as possible. We're friends. That's a great space to be in. So basically no, I don't see us getting back together."

"Does he know about me? Us being friends again?"

"Well, of course he knows *of* you. Doesn't like the idea of you much, sorry to say. I first met him a few days after I last saw you in Kiev when I was still reeling in post–breakup frustration, so his impressions come from that time, unfortunately. He knows our history, or at least the general story. But no, he doesn't know you're here now, if that's what you mean. I didn't see the need."

We stared across the coffee table at each other. I could already feel the wine massaging its relaxing effect into every part of my body. I knew that I needed to be careful.

He stayed for a couple more hours, shuffling ever closer as we talked. There was something intoxicating about his presence; that direct connection to who I was in the past. I was tremendously naïve back then to be sure, but there was a time when he and his country and his family's cottage in the countryside and his mother and the food and the adventure of it all had thrilled me endlessly. But what had been missing all along was substance and honesty, and I must never forget that. Nostalgia is a seductive liar, as someone once said, however much the romantic in me wanted to believe otherwise, even now.

Józef looked at the time on his phone, and stood up. He yawned and smiled, helped take the bottle and glasses to the kitchen, and then walked with me to the door. A hug, an exchange of superficial parting pleasantries, and that was it.

I'll admit: deep down my ego had been quietly promoting the fantasy of him suddenly realising what he'd lost in me all those years ago. In this reckoning, he'd throw himself into my arms and beg me to let him make amends for all those long–ago wrongs of immature youth.

But imagination and reality are not *always* the best of bedfellows. Of course, he did no such thing. As ever, I found his thoughts and his intentions as inscrutable as his expression.

With a perplexing sense of anti–climax, Józef headed back to his hotel. He left early the next morning, even before I'd got the kids off to school.

Perhaps it was just as well. Józef was a dangerous slope that I knew better than to climb.

CHAPTER EIGHTEEN

On a bright August evening during one of our regular late night phone chats, Andy gleefully told me about a competitor of his who was retiring. This guy had called Andy out of the blue to offer him his business for the equivalent of a third of a year's income.

I'll admit, my first instinct was one of unsupportive horror. Andy had never been great with managing money, and I knew absolutely that his share of the house money had been slowly chipped away at by daily restaurant meals, a new computer, gaming equipment, and endless cups of take–away coffee. He already owed quite a few thousand on his car and business loans. Combined with this was his habitual disinclination for hard work. I just couldn't see how he'd cope with four hundred more clients to take care of, no matter how well–intentioned. If he bought this business and it failed, as I really feared it would, Andy would lose absolutely everything: his money, his self–respect, his reputation, his future. I was doubly–stunned to learn that our lawyer – who I'd really believed to be a very practical, no–risk type – was openly enthusiastic about the proposal. He'd heartily agreed with Andy that this would be a wonderful opportunity, and that he should go for it.

I tried very hard to talk Andy out of it. But this just irritated him into insisting that he'd be going forward with the deal and it was nothing to do with me. It was too good of an opportunity to pass up, he said, and he'd somehow figure out the money part.

His reaction was a sharp reminder that he was right about one thing: I no longer had a say in his decisions. Where once I'd have pushed and persuaded and probably had my way, I now had to just back off and leave things to him and to fate. It was a bittersweet pill to swallow.

Around this same time, I was getting frustrated again at the lack of information coming from Pavel. I'd heard about other people who'd applied at the same time as us receiving their visas. Our case was fairly straightforward, the paperwork nightmare aside. I'd have thought we'd have heard something by now.

But nothing.

I got in touch with Pavel, who reluctantly offered to stop by later that afternoon after meeting another client. Presumably a rich Russian with no children.

I waited an hour longer than he'd promised, and was just leaving to get the boys from school when he finally turned up.

"What's the update on the visas? Will I receive them soon?" I demanded almost crossly.

Pavel cleared his throat nervously.

"I have letter from the police," he informed me. "Your visa is processed."

"Great!"

"But... there is sixty–day delay from date of your visa for your children."

"Why?"

"In Slovak law, police cannot process the child application before the parent."

I shook my head in confusion. "I don't understand. Their applications were in the same file."

"Yes."

"So... I don't get it."

Pavel stared back at me, barely blinking. He handed me an official–looking letter, printed from top to bottom on both sides of the page.

Although I couldn't read Slovak, something did catch my eye. "Pavel, when did you get this letter?"

Pavel shifted uncomfortably from one foot to the other, and forced a small cough.

I leaned forward, skimming the page of unintelligible Slovak legalese, trying to make sense of it.

"This is dated two months ago."

"I forgot. I receive many, many documents."

Not even a hint of a fake sorry, the weasel. I was beyond furious at his spectacular ineptitude.

"So, basically, the officer picked up the boys' applications first, saw mine under theirs, and realised they could buy themselves a bit of time with this loophole," I fumed. "Is that what you're saying?"

Pavel shrugged. "It could be."

"You should have told me. I would have been prepared. Now, I have to worry for two more months."

"It's normal in Slovakia. Alien police do not have the budget; they are understaffed."

I was beyond livid, and he needed no fluency in English to know it.

"Pavel. I'm sorry. But this is where I'm going to lose my shit. I've paid you a fortune, and I want an answer. I'm tired of all the delays. I'm tired of chasing you for answers. I'm tired of all the confusing answers when you do answer. That letter was the last straw for me. I don't care what you need to do to get an update. But I want you to do it."

Pavel called me to meet with him outside his office a couple of days later. Without a word, he handed me a piece of paper. It was a couple of short paragraphs and a signature.

"What's this?" I demanded, gearing up for round two.

"Confirmation document. I received today. Police cannot give visas same day. But now they process your kids' visas. In two weeks, they will be ready, I'm sure." There was a slight hint of relief in his tone. Slight, but I silently allowed the possibility that it was there.

I squinted at Pavel in the afternoon sun, all manner of sarcastic observations ready to fly from my lips. But, I'd got what I wanted. He was clearly never going to be great at this, so all I could do was hope that this would be resolved quickly, and then warn others. And, of course, find a new lawyer next time around.

To our mutual relief, when we met again ten days later, Pavel was able to hand over the three plastic purple–and–pink temporary residency cards. I was so delighted that I almost hugged him. Somehow, though, I managed to restrain myself.

Moving more quickly than I'd ever have given him credit for, Pavel jumped back in his car and drove off as speedily as he could.

Now that the cards had been issued, I had three days to provide the police with proof of health insurance for us all, and thirty days to complete full medical examinations at a government–approved facility. Then, the process would be complete – and I could wave an extremely hearty good–bye to Pavel. No doubt the feeling would be more than mutual.

Ján had offered to help me deal with the health insurance company, which needed to be done in person. Unfortunately, he'd been ill several times over the past few weeks, so I was reluctant to bother him.

Brisk, efficient, and quasi–fascinated by it all despite her adamant declarations to the contrary, Michaela swiftly stepped in to help.

When we arrived at the health insurance office on Cintorínska Street, a sign taped to glass door announced that the office was closed due to a technical issue.

Without bothering to consult Pavel, we figured the three–day deadline surely wouldn't include a weekend, right? My attitude was pretty much one of 'whatever' by this point, so we took the risk, and turned up again on Monday morning rather than go somewhere else.

When our number was called, we sat down in front of the representative. She was the first smiling customer service person I'd met so far in Bratislava.

Michaela quickly filled her in. The representative smiled, and nodded, and created the policy while firing off questions in rapid Slovak.

Michaela responded just as swiftly, handing over each document as it was requested.

"Do you have notarised translations of the boys' birth certificates?" Michaela asked me.

"Of the birth certificates? No, do I need them?"

"Yes, she's saying the originals are no good."

"The alien police didn't need translations, as far as I recall. Nor did their school or anyone else. I was told the authentication stamp from the Slovak embassy in Canada was sufficient."

"Well, they do. She says on their website, there's apparently a full list of documents you need."

I quickly skimmed through the photocopied list that bloody Pavel had given me. There was absolutely no mention of a translated birth certificate.

However, no manner of persuasion, negotiation, or insistence that my lawyer had told me otherwise would budge the kindly representative's stance. She was very apologetic, but the rules were the rules.

Angry tears sprang into my eyes. I was furious with Pavel, and absolutely fed up with the never–ending issues I kept having to deal with. Every step along the way felt like a bewildering, frustrating, avoidable obstacle.

Michaela grabbed me by the arm and pulled me up with a polite "We'll be back" to the representative.

As the lady handed us back the residency cards and documents, Tom's fell to the ground at my feet. I grabbed the precious card quickly, and froze.

"Oh. My. God," I cried out loud.

"What? What?" Michaela wanted to know, staring at the card.

"The date," I near–howled, "Tom's expires in four months. Pat's and mine are in eighteen months. Why? Why?"

Michaela grabbed all three cards, hoping that I'd made a mistake. But there were the dates, in unmistakeable black–and–white.

"All I can say is, fucking Pavel," I swore.

Michaela nodded angrily.

"I just can't do this anymore," I moaned, pushing my way out of the office and into the fresh air outside. "Every single time I've dealt with the authorities or some official body, the rules have been so changeably complicated. There have been so many fuck–ups. I just can't – I'm not going through all of this again in four months. I can't, I won't. I'm not getting translations. I've had enough. If I'd known I needed translations, I'd have got them done over the weekend with plenty of time to spare. Not this ridiculous rush, with this stupid deadline. And now this," I cried, flipping Tom's card back and forth angrily between my thumb and a finger.

Michaela nodded sympathetically. "Listen to me. Pavel's office is just around the corner. Right? I'm going to speak with him."

I made incoherent splutters through bitter tears.

"No, I'm doing it. You paid him a lot of money, it's ridiculous. He should be doing his job. Let me speak to him in a language – and with language – he'll definitely understand."

She marched me along to the five–storey office building where Pavel's office address was listed. "You wait here. I'll go see if I can find him."

Michaela was gone for five or six very long minutes, during which time I was lost in miserable thoughts about the future. I had no idea where we'd go if we had to leave Slovakia. I couldn't go back to Canada so soon, tail between my legs at our new life crashing down around us. I was running low on savings thanks to Pavel and his ridiculous fee, not to mention all the other expenses involved in moving and getting settled.

Michaela soon hurried down the stairs, through the lobby, and re–joined me outside.

"OK. So, not there. Of course. I quizzed the secretary or whatever she was, but she insists he's out at a meeting somewhere. Who knows."

Michaela pulled out her phone and made a quick call while I stared at my feet. She cocked her head to one side, holding the phone between ear and shoulder as she took some notes. She then thanked the person on the other end, and hung up.

"Come on. One thing at a time. Let's deal with the translation first, then we'll figure it out about the dates. I just called a translation company up there on Grösslingová. I wrote down their address. They said the timing's tight, but they can fit it in by three o'clock if we get there ASAP. It's going to cost a little more because it's urgent, but they'll get the certificates translated and notarised so we can go back to the insurer and get the applications in by the deadline. OK? Let's go."

Without waiting for a response, Michaela grabbed my elbow, hurried me along the street, and around the corner to Grösslingová.

The translation agency was up a very short flight of steps in an old building, the scent of history rich in the dust lining the grooves and panels outside the office door.

Michaela pushed me through the door and immediately launched into a discussion with the secretary and translator, who were both standing behind the reception desk. She grabbed the documents out of my hands and handed them over, reiterated the urgency, cost, and pick–up time, and asked if they had everything they needed. The women nodded, perfectly calm and professional.

While the translator double–checked everything and the secretary called the notary to make the appointment, Michaela stepped into the hall to answer a call. When we were back outside again, she told me that George had got in touch with his lawyer, who assured him it was perfectly possible for him to sort out the permit date, and that he'd be happy to take me on as a client. He'd apparently been instrumental in sorting out some unforeseen issues for George and one of his colleagues with the alien police. He knew the officers, was familiar with the laws – and, importantly, the loopholes – and spoke good English.

Two hours later, Michaela and I went back to the agency to pick up the documents and take them to the insurance company. The boys and I were registered without further incident, and the customer service lady promised that our cards would be ready to collect within a week.

"Just finish the insurance and medical stuff with Pavel," Michaela advised as we knocked back coffee at Cukráreň Laurent to celebrate.

We'd been eyeing the rows of delectable cakes and tarts for some time while making half–hearted declarations of diets and the gym, but neither of us had yet given in.

"You're nearly at the end with him now, so there's no point paying someone else for that. Insurance is done, and the medicals are stupid but easy. Pavel just has to hand in your insurance confirmation and medical reports, and that's it. George's lawyer can take over from there. I promise you, he'll take care of everything, and quickly. I hear he's amazing."

I was elated. "Thank you *so* much. This has been an incredibly frustrating process. You've been fantastic."

"No problem," Michaela smiled. "Haven't you wondered why I like meeting up with you? How else am I supposed to keep entertained with the latest plot twists of Pavel & Co.?"

I smirked. "I'm so glad to be a source of amusement."

"Come on. Let's get some cake," Michaela capitulated. "We'll bill Pavel for it later."

CHAPTER NINETEEN

On an unexpectedly chilly morning in mid–September, Ján and I were practically hugging our coffees in Mon Dieu. It was nearly full, and the only free table was a just–vacated spot by the door. We quickly took it, two seconds ahead of another pair who turned immediately back into the wind to find somewhere else to eat. The windows inside were a touch steamy; a reminder of the impending autumn.

I was thoroughly drained on that particular day, and mentioned it casually almost as soon as we sat down. The stress I'd been under those past few months was beginning to crush me. I was generally worn out by solo–parenting and the ongoing visa issues. I had been putting myself under a huge amount of pressure to keep a regular income coming in with my project work, which entailed many late nights as my clients were in different time zones. Individually, I could handle those issues. But Dušan's behaviour was adding an unpredictable dimension to my anxiety. The night before, he had been on the premises until late into the evening, first discussing repairs with the contractor, then showing some guests into one of the apartments, then cleaning another, and then lurking around without a guessable purpose in the courtyard beyond my window. It got to the point where I didn't know if he was really still out there, or if the little sounds that I heard in the darkness were the product of my on–edge imagination. Needless to say, I couldn't fall asleep until hours beyond midnight, and then was awoken at five o'clock by the boys arguing over their Lego. I had almost cancelled coffee with Ján that morning out of sheer exhaustion, but with Dušan's presence being so erratic, I had to stay out somewhere.

Here I was, a grown woman, scared to go out and scared to go home every day. I felt the children were safer when they weren't there, but that *I* was safer when they were. Being hyper alert 24/7 was draining me. I was on constant tenterhooks, straining to hear solid leather shoes pounding through the courtyard or the sound of his voice before he got close enough to catch me unawares. I was afraid to fall asleep at night, and shook with nerves as I got the kids quickly ready for school each day so we could get the hell out of there. Who could protect me? Although friends were concerned, and felt for me and gave advice, I was thoroughly aware that I lacked physical protection. No wonder I turned to wine at night to give me a little relief; to temporarily persuade me that I was being ridiculous and that he was harmless. Then the morning would come and I began looking forward to night again, when the wine would soothe it all away. And, with the drinking came nibbling, and with the nibbling came some weight gain.

Physically, I was beginning to feel as sensitive and irritable as I did mentally. I knew I couldn't go on like that. It wasn't what I moved there for. I just couldn't find a way to take control, and I was terrified. The non– Dušan issues only compounded my sense of absolute helplessness.

To be honest, I was semi–expecting sympathy or at least quiet nodding of the head from the mild–mannered Ján. He was very much into the outdoors and physical exercise, so it came as no surprise that he had an opinion to voice on the subject of health. But I wasn't expecting such a concerned reaction. To be fair, I had only mentioned the excessive wine and lack of sleep the previous night to him; my fears about Dušan were still too raw that morning to verbalise so soon.

"You should take better care of your health," he admonished me with some energy. "Drinking and not enough exercise is not good for your health. You should not drink so much, and you should also get more sleep. Maybe you should do some yoga or jogging. Or Pilates," he added, reeling off some of his favourite activities. "It's not good to live like this."

I was taken aback by his tone and the unexpected directness. I'd never heard him talk like that before. But… he was right. On a practical survival level, I knew very well that he was absolutely right.

I felt thoroughly mortified by my confession, but even more so by how I'd been handling the stress. While my reasons were valid, I was ashamed by how I'd stood back and let my physical and mental health slide before my very eyes. I was a *mess*. I'd lived and worked in seven different countries, and life had thrown me plenty of challenges. I could not, would not, let these temporary setbacks bring me down any more.

As I worked through the crimson of embarrassment while Ján quietly observed me over his espresso, I silently vowed to stop using wine as a crutch. I'd join the gym, and, most importantly, I'd come up with an action plan to face each challenge one by one.

Into my head popped a Gene Krantz quote that had often inspired me in the past. *Let's work the problem, people. Let's not make things worse by guessing.* So, I'd work the problem. If Krantz's team could bring the badly–damaged Apollo 13 back to Earth against all those incredible odds, I could surely figure out my own personal challenges and overcome them. I would not let myself sink any deeper. My boys were relying on me.

Ján walked me home after we finished our coffee. Aware of my fear of Dušan, he kept an eye out from the roadside entrance until I was safely in my apartment with the door locked behind me. I then threw myself face–down on the sofa bed and sobbed heartily, before falling into a deep mid–morning slumber.

That night, when the kids were finally asleep in their shared bed, I sat down at the table with a raspberry tea. In front of me was an A4 notepad. I firmly divided a clean page into two columns with a black ballpoint pen. In the first column, I bullet–pointed every issue, from the biggest to the most minute. In the other, I jotted down everything I could think of to tackle these issues, numbering the most probable as I went along. I worked at it for a good hour, adding more detail and refining the action plan as the rational side of me kicked in.

Once I was finally done, I carefully looked back over what I'd written. The list ran to fourteen items. With each of these now reduced to a black–and–white summary, they suddenly felt very possible to overcome.

Now I just needed to pull myself together, stay cool, and work the problem. I would not let myself down.

CHAPTER TWENTY

Although Tom's permit date had yet to be sorted out, we still had to get our medicals done within the original thirty days. To this end, my dear friend Pavel arranged for his assistant, Iveta, to book and go along to the appointments with us.

We arrived at the clinic at 8am. Although it was quite early, there were six or seven people ahead of us in the minimalist 1950s–style waiting room. From snippets of overheard conversation, I guessed them to be mostly Russian and Ukrainian.

There was a persistent smell of urine in the room, very reminiscent of cat piss. No matter where we sat, the stench followed.

Pat and Tom played with a pile of toys in the corner while we waited for our names to be called by the nurse with her authoritative clipboard. They'd never seen toys in a waiting room before. The public health and medical offices on Prince Edward Island that we had been to had long ago removed them for fear of germs. The parent in me couldn't decide whether to be pleased or alarmed.

Iveta explained in good English that urine samples would be taken first. When we were called up by the clipboard, we duly left ours in self–labelled tubes with the dozen or so others already sitting in the sample holder, a grossly fascinating collection of motley yellows.

A few minutes later, we were summoned individually into a little white room to have blood samples taken. I went first, then came along with each unsuspecting child as they slid into the chair and were pounced upon quickly by the nurse and her needle.

Tom, ever the stoic, bit his lip and nodded red–faced at her soothings in Slovak as he held back his tears.

Pat, on the other hand, bellowed "Ow, that hurt! You tricked me!" in theatrical outrage, making me and the nurse giggle in spite of ourselves.

We were then directed back to the pee–scented waiting room, where we sat down for another quarter of an hour until our names were called for our interview with the doctor. I use the word 'interview' lightly.

The doctor was a middle–aged woman with a kindly air and reasonable English. She waved me to take a seat, and let the boys touch her wall map of the world while telling them the Slovak names of each country they pointed to. She then indulgently answered their million–and–one questions about her job and equipment for some minutes, smiling at their enthusiasm.

This was all very well and delightful, but we'd been in her office for ten minutes and nothing remotely medical–related was happening. I was keen to get the kids off to school, and even more desperate for coffee. It took another five minutes of chit–chat before the doctor brought out her clipboard.

"How much do each of you weigh?" she asked.

I had no idea.

"It doesn't matter," the doctor replied with a relaxed smile. "We can estimate. Do you know your heights?"

"Unfortunately, not off the top of my head. Sorry."

She waved her hand and wrinkled her nose in a not–to–worry gesture, and jotted down her best guesses. I could have wondered why she didn't just take these measurements herself, as they had scales in the other room and surely someone had a measuring tape in a medical centre? But I knew better than to propose such logical assumptions.

"Any diseases? Broken bones? History of family illness?"

No, no, and no.

"Are you all in good health?"

Pat had the tail–end of a sniffle, but there was no way I was going to admit that.

"No, we're all very healthy. Almost too healthy."

The doctor nodded. "Is there anything else I should know?" she asked in conclusion.

I shook my head. She put down her pen, smiled at the boys, and the interview was complete.

The doctor patted the kids on the head as I ushered them out to re–join Iveta, who walked with us across the road to the clinic where the x–ray would be carried out.

Iveta led us through the small foyer, turned to the right, and guided us down a narrow corridor. She stopped at a small counter and handed our IDs to the orderly behind the sliding window. He sighed, and tap–tapped our information slowly into his computer while muttering a one–sided monologue that Iveta was doing her nervous best not to laugh at. The orderly then rolled his eyes, handed over the IDs, and slammed the window shut again.

"What was that all about?" I asked as Iveta walked us to the x–ray cubicles at the end of the corridor.

She blushed. "He thinks foreigners only come to our country to sell drugs," she admitted. "I told him he is wrong, and he said I'm saying that because I want your drugs. He was so serious, it was very strange, and funny."

"Yeah dude, that's precisely why I came to Slovakia and went to all this expense and trouble. Just so I could sell drugs," I scorned, incredulous. It was an unfortunate attitude in someone in direct and influential interaction with foreigners.

The x–rays were straightforward. I went in first to get a feel for what was to come, and then went with each child as they did theirs. The x–ray machine was a monster, like the pictures I'd seen of early computers in the 1950s.

A nurse came into the sparse dark room, instructed each of us in turn to strip to the waist in a small side cubicle, pressed the cool flat panels of the clunky machine against our backs and chests, and ducked inside a shielded control cubicle during the ten–second *whirr–beep* that followed. We were then sent back into the cubicle to dress, and that was that.

We parted from Iveta on the street outside the x–ray department. The entire medical had taken less than an hour to complete, although it felt much longer. I was puzzled yet somehow unsurprised by the farcical nature of the exams. At €200 apiece the experience wasn't cheap, either. But they were a necessary part of the permit process and, if nothing else, would make for a great conversation starter.

Iveta told me she'd pick up our reports as soon as they were ready, and give these to Pavel to deliver to the alien police.

"Thank you, Iveta," I told her with a sincere shake of the hand. "You've been the most efficient part of this entire permit process."

Iveta smiled and went on her way. I took the boys to school via Praclík for a breakfast of fresh pretzels.

As we crossed the road near the school, with Tom already on the pavement and me pulling Pat along with one foot still on the road, a shiny black jeep screeched to a halt close by the curb. I'd seen it coming along, appearing to speed up as the driver spotted us. Distracted by both children nattering at the same time, I hadn't been too worried though as we were so close to the pavement.

The boys squealed with fright as the jeep skidded up, and clutched my hands tightly as we all stared wide–eyed at the car. The driver screamed at me for a good thirty seconds, ranting and cursing and doing a Robert de Niro fingers–to–his–eyes–then–my–eyes style gesture as he roared. Other pedestrians crossed the road and walked by as this was happening, rubbernecking to get a good view as they hurried away, but no one dared intervene.

The driver continued to shout through the window, obviously high on something. His pretentious wife, having had too much surgery to move much of her face let alone open her mouth, simply looked on with no obvious emotion. It didn't take any Slovak language to realise that he was trying to falsely accuse us of walking in front of his car. Red–faced with rage at the polite derision of my expression as I unfroze and began tugging the boys away, the driver unbuckled his seat belt viciously and made as if to get out of the car.

The boys were frightened, so I calmly turned my back on the jeep and hurried them along, desperately hoping he'd just leave us alone. We were very close to the school; within running distance if it came to that.

"Mummy, why was he so angry?" Tom gasped, as the jeep sped away with split–second blares of the horn, one after angry one.

"Some people just have a hard time being nice," I explained away lightly, heart racing with adrenaline. "Maybe he's having a bad day. Just ignore him, baby. Let's go tell your friends and teachers all about the fun morning you had at the clinic!"

What a morning. And it had barely yet begun.

CHAPTER TWENTY-ONE

After not hearing a word from Józef in weeks, and not even expecting to hear from him again to be honest, I was surprised by his familiar voice on the other end of the line.

"How are you?"

"I'm good, thanks. You?"

"Everything's great."

"You've been quiet," I observed.

"I've been busy with client projects. Training sessions. Travelling. And I've taken up basketball and tennis again. Actually, I've entered a few competitions."

"Really? Have you won any yet?"

"Frankly, no. I tell myself it's just for fun, to improve my game. Then I don't feel so annoyed for not winning. But I've come third twice."

"Well, that's pretty good. You're being modest."

"Third is not winning. But it's a start. I could enjoy this lifestyle. Women admiring me from the side-lines, the prizes, staying in different places to participate in competitions."

"Like you don't have enough admiring women as it is," I joked.

"It's a hard life, I know it."

We fell silent. I had a feeling that I knew the answer to the question that hung unarticulated between us.

"And so? Are you back together?"

"Well. Actually. Yes."

"Since when?"

"Two, three weeks. We're living together, most of the time. She still has her apartment from her parents. She stays there sometimes, but will rent it out for extra income."

I was stunned, remembering his opinion about the situation when we last spoke. "I guess... I do, I do congratulate you both."

"Thank you."

"What made you change your mind?"

"It turns out that the grass is not so green on the other side for her. She had two short relationships. They were too much work. She heard I'd gone on some dates, nothing significant, but it seems she didn't like that. So, she decided we should try to make it work. She asked me to change some things. Some very superficial things, in my opinion, but it makes her happy."

"You mean, she wanted her jam as well as her bread. Or maybe you did."

"Perhaps it's because I should be a good example to my kid."

Neither of us spoke for several long moments.

I don't really know why I cared or felt so cross. I knew for sure that I didn't love him, as much as he didn't love me. Perhaps I was angry on her behalf, as a woman. Perhaps I was a little jealous of how easily he moved in and out of relationships. Perhaps, my heart whispered, my ego was more than a little bruised by how he had never appreciated me; that I was considered less pursuable than all these other women he seemed to only superficially connect with.

"It wasn't an easy decision."

"I can imagine. Tell me this. Are you happy?"

"Well, it's rather boring and stable," he chuckled. "But it's familiar, and almost everyone approves. What else could I do?"

"What do you mean?"

"My question to myself was, what's the long–term alternative? The saying that rings here is, 'If I knew that my third wife would be like the second, I would have stayed with the first'."

"That's horribly cynical, don't you think?"

"Is it? You're too much a romantic, and not enough a realist. Anyway, it was a nice feeling, this attention from other women in the meantime. Nothing serious, just light fun."

I was mortified at the realisation that perhaps I was just one of those women in his mind, and how little I meant to him even after more than a decade. I would never forget the excruciating awfulness of that moment.

Józef realised what he'd said.

"You take it too seriously. I probably shouldn't have contacted you. I'm sorry. We quarrelled, and you always make me feel good about myself. I needed to hear your voice, to hear you telling me I'm such a great guy." His voice was cheerful, defusing.

"As a friend, you know I'll always support you," I told him quietly and with as much dignity as I could gather. "But. This has to stop. I honestly think if you see a future with her, you should really just focus on that and stop wondering what else is out there and be a good, loyal husband. But if you stay because it's convenient and socially acceptable, that's honestly not a great thing to do unless she feels the same way. That's for you both to decide. I'm sorry to be harsh, but you have a lifelong habit of running away when women want more from you. Or you take what they give until you get bored or go too far outside your comfort zone. It must have been an absolutely shocking experience for someone to leave you for a change."

"Funny."

"No. I'm very serious. I applaud her bravery in leaving you last year. As someone who cares about you, all I can say is hopefully she loves you, if she came back. Do the right thing by her. Don't casually use me as an ego–stroker. That's not fair to me. I've consistently forgiven your behaviour to me in the past and I've always looked for the best in your motives. How horribly practical of me," I added with a self–deprecatory laugh. "I'm hugely grateful for how you've influenced my life over the past year, whether you meant to or not. Perhaps that was the reason you were sent back into my life. And now, it's time to move on."

I could hear by the amused sighs that he wasn't taking my sermonizing too seriously. He ended the call with good–humoured best wishes, and hung up.

I stared into space for minutes afterwards, trying to figure him out. But it was no use. His views on love were bafflingly alien to mine. I would never understand him. Perhaps I simply wasn't meant to.

CHAPTER TWENTY-TWO

"Goodbye."

Dušan stood up with a smile, holding out his long arms for a hug.

He had stopped by to collect that month's cash portion of the rent while the boys were at school. He then sat about on the sofa for far longer than I was comfortable with, making drawn—out small talk about my work and the weather and how we should really meet up for that wine one night soon as he counted out each note carefully before writing me a receipt.

I was very reluctant to give him a hug, but he leaned forward with practised speed and wrapped me in an inescapable clutch. I tried not to shudder, repelled by his sweaty warmth and the scent of his aftershave, both forced upon me by my damn politeness.

He sniffed my hair, and kissed the crook of my bare neck, and ran his hand down to the small of my back, all so swiftly that I almost doubted these things were actually happening.

Instinct kicked in: scared and trapped and cognisant of his superior strength, I struggled to get away from him.

In a flash, he moved his hands and converted his grasp to a regular hug, before letting me go.

Were it not for the pressure I could still feel on my neck and lower back, I could easily have convinced myself that I had imagined everything.

Dušan, for his part, acted as if absolutely nothing untoward had occurred.

I stepped away, spluttering out a "Please don't do that!"

He looked very confused. "What do you mean?"

I stared at him, dumbfounded.

"You don't like hugs?" he continued.

Blushing and quivering, I didn't know what to say. Had I misinterpreted it?

"I hope you don't think something?" Dušan enquired. His tone was mildly perplexed, but the undertone was unmistakeable.

Terrified by the sudden shift in atmosphere, all I could focus on was that we were all alone. I had nowhere to run. I had to find a way to get out of this.

Breaking away from his gaze with a neutralising smile and an "Of course not," I cautiously stepped around him and opened the door between the living room and the vestibule.

As I did so, I deliberately looked at the open window less than two metres to my right. I could hear approaching voices out there, reassuring in their safe proximity.

Dušan picked up his satchel and followed me to the door.

"I am very sorry. I think you think something of me," he sombrely declared. "Slovak people are very friendly. I just want you to feel welcome. To stay in our apartment is like staying in our home. You imagine perhaps more than I mean. Next time, we just shake hands. OK?"

He strode past me in a huff, down the two steps into the vestibule, out the front door, and down the outer stairs.

I locked the door as quickly as I could behind him, pushing a chair against it just in case.

After that, I no longer felt safe in the apartment. Even with the kids there after school, playing and jostling with not a care in the world, I was deeply uneasy. I couldn't leave the blinds open, as the bottom of the windows were at head height for anyone walking by. I found myself frequently glancing with fear at the bell above the living room door, afraid that at any moment it would give its tinny *burrp* and Dušan would be back. My nerves were raw with tension, my ears constantly straining to assess how far away he was whenever his voice echoed across the car park while escorting guests to their units.

That night, I propped an umbrella, toys, and a windchime against the front door – anything portable that would noisily alert me if someone tried to enter while we slept. I then strewed Lego pieces and Hot Wheels cars around the door for good measure. I left the key inside the door, making it difficult for anyone to open it with a key from the other side. Despite the stuffiness of the autumn evening in that cramped apartment, I closed all the windows.

Unsurprisingly, sleep was a very long time coming. It was past 4am when my eyes finally closed. The boys sprang out of bed and clambered into mine a little over two hours later. How was I going to get through the day? I felt like I was at breaking point.

I called Michaela from the safety of a park bench along the Danube once I'd dropped the boys off at school.

"You should report the creep."

"He hasn't done anything police report–worthy."

"It's only a matter of time."

"Don't say that."

"No, seriously. He knows exactly what he's doing. He's playing the innocent nice guy thing, but he knows. I bet it's not the first time."

"I don't think so, either. He's too deliberately innocent. Even if he's just terrible with boundaries, it's scaring the hell out of me. I need to get out of that place. I wanted to check with you, could you keep an eye out for anything, and let me know?"

"I'm onto it. Actually, I do have a two–bedroom near the presidential palace, in fact very close to where you are now. The rent is €60 less, and it's available immediately. I've seen it, it's very nice. You'd like it. The good news is, the owner lives in Prague, so he's never here."

"He lives in Prague? Perfect. I'll take it."

"Let's go check it out first," Michaela replied. "Just to be sure. I'm pretty sure the owner will be happy to rent it without meeting you, because I can give a personal recommendation. But you should see it first. I can meet you at nine tomorrow if you like?"

"Yes, I like. Very much."

The next morning, after another night of terrible sleep but thankfully no sign of Dušan, I dropped the kids off at school and sped back to meet Michaela outside the Austrian Cultural Forum off Hodžovo námestie. The apartment was just a very short walk from there.

Michaela pulled the building key out of her pocket and let us in to the foyer. I followed her up a short flight of broad grey stone stairs to the first floor. She then took out another key, inserted it, turned it twice, and pushed open the dark wooden door of the apartment at the very top of the stairs.

Strangely, my first impression was one of nostalgia and uncertainty. Built in the 1930s, the scent took me straight back to Józef's family's cottage in the countryside.

For the past two years the apartment had lain empty, as the son had had no time to travel from Prague to Bratislava to clear out his late father's possessions. It had therefore been poignantly suspended in time, with the dust blanketing the furniture and jars in the cupboards remaining undisturbed until now. Yet despite its eeriness, the apartment felt very serene.

"The guy who lived here – his family were important political influencers and historians in Slovakia," Michaela whispered, as if she might be overheard by the dead. "The owner's grandfather moved in here first with his family, but they were exiled, or went into exile, or something like that, to Germany. After communism, I'm not sure what happened, but I think the grandson said the family came back to Bratislava and then returned to Germany. His son – the one who lived here until he died two years ago – again I'm not exactly sure of the story, but he moved to Canada with his wife and kids and stayed for thirty years. From what I understand, he then came back to Slovakia and lived here permanently, but was visiting family in Canada when he died. Anyway, I think that's the story I heard. Like I said, the grandson who owns this place now is in Prague. He lived in Canada as a child and came back with his father. When Czechoslovakia separated, he moved to Prague. This place is basically just income. Apparently, he inherited a few properties here and in Prague and in Canada too. Lovely, lovely guy. You'd never see him, which is actually what you want after the whole Dušan drama."

Michaela enthusiastically ran through her realtor spiel as I wandered through the rooms. The place was light and airy and beautifully warm. It was tremendously peaceful, despite a kindergarten being directly below. Through the sitting room windows, I could see straight into the neighbouring church. Although nearly within sight of the presidential palace and all the traffic that flowed around it, the apartment was silent, welcoming. The very opposite of where I was now.

"The grandson just finished doing the place up. New flooring, carpets, kitchen unit, see? There's a new washing machine and dryer over there in the main bedroom. A dishwasher here in the kitchen. I know you want a dishwasher."

I smiled. "Hey, you got me at "you'd never see him"".

Michaela grinned. "And the bonus is the erotic 'supermarket' just down the street."

"I wonder if they do loyalty cards, like other supermarkets?"

"I'm not sure that's something I'd want to keep in my wallet. So anyway, you'll take it?"

"The apartment? Yes, absolutely."

"Excellent. I spoke to the guy on the way here. He said if you decide to go ahead, he'll be here in a few days and you can sign the contract then. He'll hold the apartment for you until then."

"Yes, please. Let's do it."

While Michaela put in a call to get the ball rolling, I peered out the windows at the garden behind the church. I had a very good feeling about this place.

Everything happened just as Michaela had predicted. The owner gave his immediate go–ahead, and Michaela got going on the paperwork. The owner and his uncle would travel to Bratislava a day or two before the move to do some small renovations, and officially give me the keys at the same time. If everything went to plan, it would be mine in seven days.

To celebrate, Michaela and I grabbed a bite to eat, followed by a coffee from Pán Králiček.

She then walked part of the way home with me. "OK. Go. Don't be afraid. Deal with Vilma. Give her notice immediately. Not to Dušan, OK? And don't let Vilma make you feel guilty. She should know what Dušan's like. He can't be allowed to do this to anyone else, 'innocent' or not."

"You're right. I'm hoping he's not meaning to be as creepy as he's coming across. He definitely has some serious personal space issues, if nothing else. But, not my monkeys, not my circus, and all that."

Michaela rolled her eyes at my optimistic theory, and shooed me on my way.

As soon as I got home, I quickly went to the bathroom, then flopped into a chair, picked up my phone, and scrolled through until I found Vilma's number. *Here goes*, I thought, taking a deep breath. I felt tremendously nervous. I had decided to just give Vilma notice without going into detail. If Dušan was scared off enough to never do it again, I didn't want to cause him any trouble.

Just before I hit the call button, however, a soft *scritch–scratch* in the direction of the front door caught my ear. Curious, I got out of my chair and tip–toed over to investigate. There had been workmen out there for most of the morning, installing a new camera system for a business on the side of the courtyard leading to the street. They'd been sitting on my front steps when I came home, eating their lunch and smoking cigarette after cigarette. I didn't want them hanging around and leaving ash by my doorway, but I figured they would provide plenty of protection if Dušan turned up again.

My eyes were abruptly bewitched by the keyhole. The silver key I'd left in the door was twitching ever so slightly, and most definitely unnaturally. I could hear metal scratch against metal; a key on the outside grating against mine, making it jerk.

Dušan. It could only be.

Petrified and trapped, I knew my only option was to take him by surprise and confront him. I banged on the door and shouted at him to stop, which he immediately did. I turned the key and threw open the door with a bang.

On the doorstep, Dušan looked up at me, moderately startled. He clearly hadn't anticipated me being there, as I was normally out at this time of day. But it was equally obvious that he wasn't too concerned.

"Can I help?" I demanded with false bravado.

Dušan shook his head and pushed past me, seemingly oblivious to my attempt to block his entry before he'd answered my question. He was clutching a large water container in his long–fingered hands.

"My workmen need water to mix cement," he told me. "I will be fast." Uninvited, he took the container to the bathroom, where a bra and underwear were hanging over the drying rack against the wall.

But the space between the tap and the container hole was too tight, so he took the container to the kitchen instead.

I deliberately left the front door open, and ran into the kitchen.

"This is not OK."

Dušan wasn't listening.

"This is *not* OK," I repeated, with tears of fearful indignation.

He continued to ignore me.

The container now full, and thoroughly unconcerned, Dušan gave the merest of apologies for bothering me as he screwed the lid on and strode past. On the doorstep, he turned back for the briefest of seconds. The look he shot me was an unspoken, utterly clear warning. This was his home, and he would do whatever he liked. Whenever he liked. However he liked.

I had nowhere to hide.

I had a sudden flashback to a long-repressed memory. A hotel room in Germany. The male owner of the husband–and–wife establishment had entered my room to inspect the heater. It was summer; the heaters were not in use. He'd been eyeing me for a couple of days, making me feel increasingly uncomfortable. I was therefore very thankful to be leaving that morning. I'd just finished packing and was taking my time to check out, as the train at the nearby station wouldn't depart for another half–hour. The husband ignored my request to come back after I'd gone, and invited himself in. He closed the door behind him, his eyes flicking between me and the bed. I knew what he was thinking: how best to get me there without a struggle. Had I not faux–casually picked up my bag as he pretended to inspect the heater, and scurried out of there without checking out, I was 100% convinced he would have raped me.

Hyper-sensitised by this memory, I acted swiftly. Heart racing, primal fear governing my every breath as I focused on the here–and–now, I locked the door behind Dušan and raced to the table. I grabbed my phone and scrolled through the contacts list.

Vilma's phone rang for a few seconds before going straight through to voicemail. As hastily as possible, in case Dušan returned, I breathlessly gave my verbal notice, outlining the inappropriate touching, and the unauthorised entry moments before. I said that I would pay for that month's rent, of course, but we were moving out almost immediately. I insisted that Dušan keep his distance in the meantime.

Not ten minutes later, as I was panicking over how to get things packed as quickly as possible, the phone rang. Vilma's named flashed up on the screen, blinking accusingly. Shaking with emotion, I answered the call.

"Why didn't you tell me this before?" she instantly began. Her tone was an attempt to be both business–like and diplomatic, but the undercurrent was disbelieving fury. "It is strange that you did not say anything, and now *this*? How would you like it if I told you we found a better tenant, and we give you notice without warning?"

I had absolutely no idea what this analogy was supposed to mean.

"I heard your message," Vilma continued. "Let me be clear. My nephew is not attracted to you. Don't worry. We talk. We talk about everything. We have talked about you. I know everything about my nephew. Never did I suspect he feels anything for you. I'm sorry, you are not his type of woman, you do not attract him. Do you understand? My nephew, he is so friendly. Everybody, they love him. He has many friends. He is treating you like family. We are a very close family, very close. He is a good man. He is *not* attracted to you. You can believe me. I would know if he is. He hides nothing from me."

Angry tears flowed as I glared at the wall in mortification while listening to this diatribe.

"Let *me* be clear," I retorted, finding my voice. "I don't care if he's attracted to me or not. I don't want to be touched like that, and I certainly don't want to have someone enter my home without permission, especially the very next day after making it *very* clear that I don't like this behaviour."

"He never told me even once about this situation."

"Why would he?"

Vilma sucked in her breath with stiff displeasure.

"I feel this is strange," she retorted. "We made many efforts to help you with your police documents. Many efforts, much expense."

"I understand you're angry at the situation, but please don't misunderstand. I paid for the notary fees and would happily reimburse you for any other expense if there were any. This is not about you. It has nothing to do with you personally, I mean."

"This is my income. It has everything to do with me."

"Then next time, please warn your nephew about boundaries instead of questioning the honesty of the person telling you about it," I cried. It suddenly made me wonder about that Canadian girl who'd stayed there before me. "In the meantime, please let him know that if he attempts to enter the apartment again, or comes anywhere near me, no matter how innocent, I have the police saved on speed dial. I've informed a friend of mine about the situation, just so you know."

I grabbed my bag. "I have to go and pick my children up from school soon. I can meet you here on Friday with the keys. Does ten o'clock work for you?"

"Be there sharp, please. I am very busy." She hung up in very angry indignation, poorly masked by an attempt to sound neutral.

I shook with emotion. I just needed to get through the next few days, I told myself, and I'd be free.

CHAPTER TWENTY-THREE

Ján sent me a quick message to see if there was any progress with the new apartment. We'd been in touch the night before I'd gone to see it, but I'd been so caught up with everything that had happened since then, that I'd forgotten to update him.

I had seen him a few times since that day at Mon Dieu. Whether he had noticed or not, I'd been following his advice about my health. Even now when I was stressed to my limit, I turned to jasmine or raspberry tea – or a latte from Pán Králiček – rather than wine. I had joined a gym and spent a lot of time walking, and was slowly but surely getting into shape again.

"Yes! I'm moving in tomorrow."

"Perfect! Do you need some help?"

This was one of those moments in life when my fear of relying on someone else battled for supremacy with the voice inside my head crying out, "Yes, please!". Truth be told, I really could use the help, but I felt strangely shy about accepting it.

"Thank you. I should be OK. I should be able to get everything there in four or five trips (it's about a four–minute walk from my current place)," I messaged back. "I'll be very glad to move! The new place is bigger and the owner lives in Prague (he speaks fluent English), so it's all perfect."

"OK. But 'when something…', then give me a call."

"Thank you."

"Actually, tomorrow I should be in downtown anyway. And I am curious about your new apartment."

"If you're in town anyway, I can maybe meet you for a quick coffee if you like. I'm hoping to start moving things around 12pm or 1pm (depends on the owner, he's still finishing some minor repairs there). So maybe I can show you the new apartment at the same time."

"Great! Is 12pm OK with you? If you have to move at that time, then of course we can drink coffee later."

"Sounds good! I'll keep you updated. The new owner is lovely, but he seems not very organised. I think it might be later than 12pm/1pm before he will say OK I can come over with my stuff. So probably we'll have more than enough time for coffee."

"Great! See you tomorrow. We can meet at Urban Space near your soon–to–be–old apartment."

"Sure! See you then."

The following day, we met up at the dot of midday outside Urban Space. To my secret delight, Ján was dressed in casual clothes suitable for helping with a move, just in case. If I wouldn't accept his offer outright, it seemed he would do it by stealth. I didn't say a word, but my heart skipped with gratitude.

We got through two coffees and a lot of chatting before the owner finally texted with an update. He and his uncle were running behind schedule with last–minute renovations, and it was likely to be 3pm before they were done.

As much as he genuinely wanted to help, Ján had an appointment at 2.30pm, so he couldn't stick around longer than that. He did, however, walk me back to my old apartment to make sure the coast was clear. Although Dušan and Vilma were supposed to be out of town that day, I was on edge at the thought of them changing their minds.

And so the repairs were finally complete, and the keys were handed over. Propelled by adrenaline, I got everything moved from the old apartment to the new within an hour. I then got the empty apartment cleaned and vacuumed as speedily as possible in case Vilma or Dušan turned up. Thankfully, there was no sign of either.

With the deepest surge of relief, I locked the door behind me and hurried off to fetch the kids from school.

The rest of that day was spent in unpacking our bags and getting the boys' new bedroom set up. Everything else could be sorted out over the coming days.

That night I slept a glorious sleep, sound in the knowledge that I was safe and would never have to see Vilma or Dušan again after Friday.

At 10.07am the next morning, Michaela and I waited impatiently in the courtyard of the old apartment building for Vilma to arrive.

"Sharp," snorted Michaela, glancing at her phone. "Thought she was so busy?"

A couple of minutes later, Vilma appeared around the corner, smiling benignly at the two of us. Beside her, with more than a touch of reluctance, was Dušan.

"Wow. The *nerve!*" Michaela exclaimed under her breath.

I was livid. After everything that had happened, I couldn't believe they would be so bold as to have him at this meeting in spite of it all.

"Dušan is the property manager," Vilma explained. "Naturally, he has to be here to make sure all is according to our inventory."

Michaela was able to express her feelings far better than I could at that particular moment. Her expression made no bones about her personal disgust as we followed them inside, before glazing it over with the air of a professional realtor determined to do her job briskly and thoroughly.

Dušan sat quietly in his chair, saying not a word, but not looking particularly contrite either. He patted at his raw red nose with a tissue while sucking on a lozenger.

For my part, I refused to directly acknowledge his presence. I was shaking.

"Poor Dušan has the flu," Vilma sighed. "I will do the talking. We let him rest. So, you have found somewhere new? What street is it on?" she asked with detached politeness.

"Somewhere in the area," I replied cryptically.

Vilma nodded.

"OK, so let's get straight down to business," Michaela cut in. "We'll make sure all is here according to your inventory."

Vilma waved away the suggestion.

"No, it's not necessary," she back–tracked. "We are very trusting. If you tell us everything is here, we believe you."

"Yes, everything is here."

"Good. You see, we trust you. We communicate. This is how we work. Dušan, he will give you the deposit back."

Under the watchful gaze of his aunt and the even steelier glare of Michaela, Dušan counted out the deposit in front of us, note by involuntary note.

"You can check again," Vilma nodded at me.

"It's OK. I trust you. This is how I work," I shot back.

Michaela took the pile of notes, deliberately and loudly counting them again. She then handed me the money and pushed the refund slip towards me for my signature. That signed, Michaela grabbed my arm, united in our absolute desire to get ourselves out of there as quickly as possible.

Vilma and Dušan also stood, the latter pushed firmly behind by his determined aunt.

As we made our way towards the exit, Vilma held out her hand and placed it on my elbow.

I flinched and instinctively pulled away. Vilma quickly removed her hand and smiled again.

"Would you do us a favour?"

Oh god, another favour.

"Would you give us a 5–star rating on Trip Advisor?"

It took all of my willpower to keep a straight face.

"When we have a problem, we discuss it and try to find solutions. We want all our guests to be comfortable, to feel welcome, to have a memorable experience."

"It was certainly memorable!" I couldn't help but mutter.

"Thank you. I hope so. We do our best to be open and personal, and to discuss issues and suggestions to make it a 5–star review. It's all about communication!"

I didn't even bother responding. I shook hands with them both to keep the façade of peace, thoroughly grateful to never have to deal with either of them ever again.

Michaela and I were barely out of sight and back on the street when we exploded in flabbergasted outrage.

"What the…?"

"Can you believe it?"

"5–star review? For dubious financial affairs?"

"For groping. Definitely five stars for groping."

"I can't believe he came to the meeting!"

"At least you got your money back. I seriously thought they'd have some reason to make deductions. I was all ready to get tough with them. I'm kinda disappointed I didn't get the opportunity."

Now that it was all over, I was shaking.

"Come on, let's grab an early lunch. Flagship Restaurant?" Michaela suggested. "I don't have any other appointments, and I saw they have a good menu today."

I nodded and followed her down Poštová, waving distractedly at the grinning Oskar next to his busy coffee stand.

We sat down to a delicious meal, the flavour of which was enhanced by sheer relief. My anxiety wearing off, I joined Michaela in a very thorough dissection of every moment, inflection of voice, expression, and the sheer absurdity of it all in minute detail as we ate.

I was feeling a little shaky still when we came back out into the sunshine, so Michaela hooked an arm through mine and strolled home with me. Home to my safe, cosy, delightful new apartment.

We parted ways with a cheerful hug just outside the presidential palace.

"You know, I'd definitely leave them a review if I were you. After all," Michaela twinkled as she ran for her bus, "it's all about communication!"

CHAPTER TWENTY-FOUR

The new lawyer was absolutely terrific. I met with him at a fast–food restaurant: not, I imagined at the beginning, an auspicious start.

However, within thirty seconds of Timotej opening his mouth, I was completely sold. He was concise, kind, authoritative, and hugely knowledgeable about the process. I found myself quickly agreeing for him to be my power–of–attorney so he could deal with the change of address process with the alien police and, of course, to sort out Tom's permit. He had a pay–when–the–work–is–complete policy, unlike the more demanding Pavel, who had exhibited more energy in collecting his fee than in properly doing the work.

Timotej outlined the process for both steps, the estimated timeframe and fee, and what he'd need from me to get started. Reasonable, precise, clear.

As soon as our meeting was over, I immediately called Michaela to give her an update.

"I told you," she crowed gleefully. "Isn't he great? He'll take care of everything. Everything's going to be just fine."

"You know what?" I replied with smile. "For the first time, I really believe it might."

"Give Pavel my regards if he comes calling for more business. If he's ever looking for a house, tell him to get in touch – not."

Life began to feel so much less stressful now. I found myself paying more attention to the world around me, and really seeing things. I enjoyed taking long walks along the river or up and down random streets when I wasn't working or with the children. The old town, especially, was an eclectic diversity of old and renewed; shiny glass and modern frontages betwixt the peeling façades of their neglected neighbours. There was an uneasy harmony between the classical and the brutalist social architecture, both with equally valid claims upon the city and its history.

"Have you seen the upside-down pyramid?" Miloš asked one morning as Oskar prepared my latte.

"No, I don't think so. What's that again?"

"The Slovak broadcasting building. It's near to here. We call it the building of the century."

"Why? Is it that impressive?" I wondered.

"No," Oskar grinned. "Because it took so long to build!"

It was the first of November, and everything was pretty much closed. Everything, that is, except for cafés and bars and a few restaurants here and there that catered mainly to the tourists. And of course, Pán Králiček.

It was All Saints Day, the annual observance for saints and for the dead. In the days leading up to it, florists did a roaring trade in flowers, votive candles flew off the shelves, and cemetery groundskeepers were kept busy clearing a year's build–up of ivy and moss in readiness for the hordes of visitors.

I was giving myself a day off from client projects and the private English classes I'd begun teaching recently. I desperately needed some time to be alone, to simply *be* for a few hours without any responsibilities.

After dropping the boys off at an afternoon art camp, I chatted idly to Miloš and Eva for a few minutes about communism and coffee, then took a walk down to the riverfront.

I reached the distinctive green arches of Stary Most almost before I knew it. The remains of my latte in hand, I sauntered towards a wooden seat a third of the way along the bridge.

It was a truly gorgeous chilly day. Below me, cruise boats were docked along the old town side of the river, with visitors streaming out from Bulgaria, Romania, Serbia, Austria, Germany, and beyond even at this time of year. The milky artichoke of the Danube, insensible of its contribution to music and art and literature and history, occasionally offered up branches or well–schooled ducklings with their mamas. A tiny Austrian *polizei* patrol boat puttered steadily up the river, reactively monitoring this peaceful border region. There was plenty to keep the eye entertained.

I breathed it all in, savouring the sweet pleasure of crunching the brown sugar crystals left unstirred in the remains of the milky foam at the bottom of my cup.

A couple and their small child ambled by, probably headed for the little playground on the Petržalka side. Laughing at a private joke, the man leaned in and kissed his partner energetically on the cheek, her blonde hair catching against his lips in the breeze. They laughed again. The moment captured an elusive ideal that I yet aspired to, despite the romantic disappointments of my life thus far.

"Do you recall that night in June, upon the Danube river? We listened to a Ländler tune, we watched the moonbeams quiver. I oft since then have watched the moon, but never, love, oh! never, can I forget that night in June, adown the Danube river," I quoted towards the scurrying water.

I smiled to myself at the über–sentimentality of my mood. Perhaps I would yet love and be loved. In the meantime, my life was rich and meaningful. I certainly didn't have any right to feel sorry for myself.

I spotted an elderly lady walking slowly over the bridge, a half–dozen votive candles visible through the white shopping bag slung over her arm. I guessed she was headed to one of the city's graveyards like everyone else.

Intrigued by the cultural significance of the day, I left the river behind me and walked up to Ulica 29. augusta, where I followed the crowd into the Ondrejský cemetery.

In the afternoon light, candles twinkled and the scent of melting wax was carried gently on the breeze. Despite the sombre nature of the occasion, the cemetery was surprisingly lively, even in its hush. I don't mean to imply *lively* as in *party*, but more of an undercurrent of human energy as people paid their unafraid respects to the past and to their future.

A loudspeaker softly projected through the trees the intonations of a priest conducting a service within the Gréckokatolícka Cirkev, the Greek Catholic church. The rumble of traffic seemed to somehow halt respectfully at the gates to the cemetery grounds. Families carrying bags of candles beelined for the graves of their relatives; teenagers chatted quietly away behind their parents; nuns tended the graves of the forgotten; and young couples whispered on mobiles or pushed strollers as if taking a walk in the park. The glorious irony of full–of–life relatives trundling ancient family members along in blanketed wheelchairs to stare wide–eyed at the headstones was not lost on my sense of humour.

Between two low–hanging branches of a nearby tree, I caught sight of an elderly gentleman, his head bent in earnest prayer. I observed him as unobtrusively as possible as he leaned forward to grasp the black metal cross marking a weathered grave, swiping away tears with the underside of his Sunday–best sleeve.

I wondered with pity who it was that he was mourning for. The mother in me fancied it was the final resting place of his own mama, and my heart swelled with maternal sympathy for his presumed long–ago loss. Imagining it was one of my own boys at some long future time, I left him to his quiet sorrow, and strolled on with a full heart.

I weaved slowly along the leaf–strewn pathways for a good hour or more, soaking in the eclectic monuments and stones with inscriptions carved in Slovak, German, and Hungarian. Architects and housewives and victims of war rested in perpetuity here alongside musicians and city leaders and the tiniest of infants buried over the course of several hundred years.

It was incredibly, powerfully magical. I'd never felt that way about a graveyard before. My heart danced with joy at the sheer delight of being alive.

November had not yet finished delivering up life lessons. As I walked the boys to school through Námestie SNP one bright cool morning in the middle of the month, I was astonished by the sudden appearance of a billboard on the side of a parked truck which hadn't been there the day before. The faces of Stalin, Hitler, and a dozen citizens trapped behind barbed wire or toiling away in labour camps stared out at the modern–day pedestrians scurrying by. Above the images, the words *Komunizmus* and *Fašizmus* were emblazoned in the black Fraktur Script font generally associated with the Nazis. The circle of blood red behind a black swastika and, separately, as the backdrop to a golden hammer and sickle, were matched by the shade of the capitalised declaration *NIKDY VIAC* that linked the two eras together. The incredible thing was, not a single person aside from me and the boys paid the billboard even the slightest hint of attention.

"Who are those guys?" Pat wanted to know.

"What are those people doing behind that fence?" added Tom, pointing up at the sign.

How do you briefly condense a brutal history driven by warped ideology, into an acceptable summary for a four– and five–year–old?

"Well, those guys were bad guys a long time ago – yes, they were real – and they weren't very nice to people – no, it was a bit worse than saying mean things to them – and a lot of people had bad things happen to them – yes, the bad guys are gone now, they won't come back. Slovakia and those countries are safe now – no, putting them in the naughty corner probably wouldn't have made them listen to their mummies."

The reason for the billboard was the anniversary of the Velvet Revolution the following day. It was so called because of the non–violent overthrow of the government back in November 1989, which ended forty–one years of communist party rule in Czechoslovakia. What began as a small student protest on International Students' Day soon avalanched. It captured the sentiments of the rest of the population who, over the coming days and weeks, surged together into increasingly larger crowds to protest with all their might the bitterly unpopular totalitarian rule. Finally, on 29 December 1989, the communist era sputtered to an end with the election of a democratic President of Czechoslovakia. Three years later in Slovakia, he was replaced by the first Slovak president following the dissolution of Czechoslovakia. *Nikdy viac* – never again – summed up Slovakia's determination to never again allow such ideologies to enslave its people.

The next morning, the boys and I happened by the very same spot. Gone was the billboard. Against the wall of the Kostol Navštívenia Panny Márie church, beneath the black plaque commemorating the events of 1989, a sea of burnt–out candles in clear and red glass holders, some upturned by an overnight wind, marked the individual salutes of countless individuals. Two large green wreaths were hung against the plaque, with ribbons noting the organisations these tokens of thanks represented.

I found myself wondering about the people who'd left the candles. I guessed they were from the older generations, I mean those old enough to remember and be thankful for the overthrow of a system that made freedom of speech and individuality impossible. How incredibly different everything was in modern–day Slovakia. Despite rumours of corruption at higher levels and the occasional political spat, it was very much off the global radar. So much so, that many of my friends abroad couldn't remember if we had moved to Slovakia or Slovenia. I guess it didn't help that the flags were also fairly similar.

These moments of living history were thrilling to share with the boys. My ardent hope was that, even if they forgot the specifics of everything they saw and heard, that each little experience would influence and broaden their eventual world perspectives for the better. These were the moments that made me tremendously grateful for leaving our old life behind, when the boys were old enough yet still absorbent enough for their characters and outlooks to be shaped by the world around them.

CHAPTER TWENTY-FIVE

Andy spent the whole of December in Bratislava for Tom's birthday and for Christmas. He could spare a little longer this time because he had enough techs to cover for him on Prince Edward Island in his absence. His business was doing extremely well. He was still up to his eyes in debt, but for the first time in his life, he could see an end in very distant sight.

We decided to surprise the children by telling them he was coming on one particular date, but he would actually arrive the day before.

I duly dropped the boys off at school on the day that Andy was due, and told them I'd be bringing a surprise with me at pick–up time.

"Bratislavské rožky?" Pat wondered, imagining his favourite poppy seed rolls.

"No."

"A donut?"

"Nope. Wrong again, you greedy monkeys. It's not food. You'll find out."

As soon as they were safely deposited in their classrooms, I walked to Most SNP to catch the yellow Vienna bus.

Upon arrival at the airport, I discovered Andy's plane would be a little late. I stationed myself in the café directly opposite the arrivals door, with a perfectly clear view of the board, and pulled out my lap–top to do some work while I waited.

When he eventually came through the gate, nearly fifty minutes after landing, Andy was seriously pissed off.

"Guess what I don't have?" he exclaimed in annoyance, by way of greeting.

I shook my head.

"My luggage?" he prompted with frustrated sarcasm, waving an official piece of paper in the air.

"Ah, that's why you're late through. I was wondering."

"Yep. The suitcase is still at Heathrow. They *think*. They'll deliver it to your place tomorrow. In the meantime, this is all I have to wear,'" he grumbled, waving both hands dramatically at his crumpled trousers and shirt.

"Don't worry. You can always buy something in town if you get desperate. But hopefully they'll deliver it early enough tomorrow."

Andy went to the smokers' lounge to calm down for a few minutes before our bus left. Smartly as it turned out, I'd bought return tickets for a good hour after he was due to land, just in case.

"You look really good," Andy acknowledged with a nod, as we sat down on the bus. "You've lost weight or something." He was calmer now that he'd had a smoke.

I grinned, pleased that he'd noticed. I was feeling really great lately. Since dropping the shield of wine and all that late night snacking, getting more sleep, and going to the gym almost daily, I'd trimmed down and gained a surprising amount of energy. I still had dark circles under my eyes because I was never going to get a full night's sleep with two early–bird children. But, with the permits nearly sorted and the old apartment nightmare behind me, I was finally able to relax. I felt, for the first time in a very long time, confident and optimistic about the future.

Andy's suitcase was delivered with Austrian precision first thing the next morning, just after we walked the kids to school. He was more than a little relieved at not having to go out and spend money on winter clothes that he'd then have to lug back to Canada. There was no sign of snow yet, but it definitely felt like December.

December also meant that the Christmas markets were finally open. It was the first day of that three–week season of festive over–indulgence, and we'd promised the boys we'd take them there after school.

As we turned onto Hviezdoslavovo námestie in the early dusk, a 3D light show danced across the surface of the Slovenské národné divadlo, the national theatre building. We were greeted by the heavenly scents of mulled wine and pancakes and sausages and potato *röstis* and grilled goats cheese and all manner of sweet and savoury and greasy and in–between deliciousness. Individual huts were set up along either side of the square as far as we could see, with benches lined down the centre for people to drink and eat at. Everything was decked in wreaths and little lights. It was a heaving, buzzing, cheerful mass; mostly locals, but with a good sprinkling of German and Hungarian speakers from over the borders, as well as the usual tour groups from Asia. Christmas decorations, hats and scarves, and small gifts were displayed at this stand and that, taking advantage of the food stall crowds by enticing them to buy something while they shuffled past in their queues. I spotted Miloš between a gap in the crowd, thoroughly enjoying the leftover wine and food left on the tables. The atmosphere was incredible.

First stop: mulled wine and kid's punch. The boys had been begging me for punch since hearing about it from school friends. For no reason other than speed, we picked the stand with the smallest queue.

Pat and Tom sipped carefully at the unfamiliar hot drink as the mugs were handed over, tongues circling lizard–like to snare the floating cubes of cinnamony apple nodding on the surface. My mulled wine was also quite good. Andy wasn't a fan of hot drinks except for coffee, so he had nothing at all.

The boys' eyes were soon caught by a word they well–recognised, *palacinky* – crêpes filled with jam and lashings of whipped cream. These were followed by a plate–sized *rösti* smothered in *Tatárska omáčka*, then a cupcake apiece, and then more punch. When I was convinced that they could absolutely eat no more, they still managed to gobble up a large slice of pizza between them.

We watched some of the children's concert on a stage set up on nearby Hlavné námestie, before squeezing our stuffed ways through the throng to go home.

"I'm still hungry," Pat complained as we walked through the door. "What's for dinner?"

And thus December rolled on, with its endless opportunities for culinary over–indulgence.

While Andy was there to help out, Timotej arranged for me and the boys to do our address re–registration interview and get new ID cards at the alien police station a couple of weeks before Christmas. We were supposed to do it within five days of moving, but had no choice but to wait for an additional document from the owner of my apartment. Even for Slovaks, paperwork could be a frustratingly onerous process. Although my landlord had inherited the property two years prior, for some very complicated reason even unknown to him, one of the numerous final documents to transfer ownership through inheritance had taken many months to resolve with the authorities. I wondered if his family's complex past had anything to do with it.

Unlike the previous times we'd been to the police station, Timotej asked us to come in at 4.30pm. We were spared the wait from ridiculous–o–clock with a crowd of impatient, nervous applicants. How he'd managed to secure us tickets without going through the early–morning list hell was a question I didn't want to ask.

At that time of day the station was almost empty, aside from a very small handful of exhausted people still waiting for their turn.

We didn't have to wait very long before Timotej called me and the boys into the inner room where the police went through each application at their individual counters. Andy stayed in the waiting room so as to not complicate things by his presence.

The female officer at our counter was extremely friendly and efficient. She discussed each of the three files with Timotej, updated our address on the system, and sent us around the corner to the little booth where her colleague would take our pictures for the new ID cards.

I carefully eyed Timotej as he smoothly explained and cajoled and negotiated. Judging from their reactions, the man was extraordinary at what he did. Without resorting to flirting, he had the officer and her two female colleagues eating out of the palm of his hand. He naturally exuded a certain sort of quiet, charismatic confidence that expressed both gratefulness and respect for their work combined with the desire to make their relatively unattractive work as pleasant as possible. He knew when to keep quiet, when to offer a genuine compliment, and when to jump in and proffer information before they had to ask for it. He leveraged his encyclopaedic knowledge of laws and loopholes to spare me the fines for not re–registering within the five days. It was a magnificently mesmerising performance, as these things go.

Unfortunately, there was nothing the officer could do to change Tom's permit date on the spot. But she promised to meet with Timotej again the following day to discuss the issue when her supervisor would be present.

He also knew when to back down, and so he smiled and thanked her and promised to be there at the appointed time tomorrow.

I badly wanted to stand up and applaud the guy.

Back in the waiting room, Timotej ordered us a taxi on his phone. He then shook hands with me and Andy, patted the boys on the head, and promised to be in touch with an update in the morning.

As we waited for our taxi, I realised with astonishment that the station had closed forty–five minutes before. The officers had kept working long past home–time, presumably just for Timotej. What a contrast to Pavel.

I didn't have the energy to cook dinner after that, so we got the taxi to drop us off on Špitálska, and took the boys to the Bratislavské langoše stall on Kamenné námestie for a quick bite to eat. It was a greasy meal that I didn't let them have that often, but I was willing to make an exception today.

It was fascinating to watch the young *langoš* maker as he quickly flicked out the dough into a rough circle until there were transparent patches he could almost see through. He then slid the 8–inch wide circle into the bubbling oil and left it to float for a few minutes until it had turned a crusty caramel. He flipped it over carefully and let it fry to a lighter shade on the other side. A long–handled fork removed the dough from the oil, when it was rapidly brushed with garlic butter and generously stodged with grated cheese. Finally, he folded the deep–fried disc of greasy gloriousness in half, holding it in place for a few moments until the cheese melted. Then, and only then, was it slid into a modest square of paper and handed over for the boys to devour with their mouths as enthusiastically as their eyes had done.

Christmas that year was completely and utterly uneventful. The kids had the excitement of their school Christmas performance at the theatre inside the Tatra Hotel before enjoying a week off. Andy was kept busy with supervising his technicians from afar as they worked their way through the hectic retail season back on Prince Edward Island. My client project work never stopped, but it was all fairly routine.

Christmas Day came and went, low–key and humdrum. Andy had never been a fan of Christmas or Easter or birthdays or celebrations in general. So long as the boys had a good time and got some gifts, he otherwise didn't think too much about it. Which meant that in the end, I was the one who went out and bought both of us some small gifts. Maybe it seemed superficial, but somehow it was important to me that the boys grew up never questioning the importance of acknowledging their partner in this way.

This visit was emotionally smoother than the last had been. By this stage, we both felt we'd been successful in forging our separate lives. The boys still had no idea we were separated, but we'd begun dropping gentle hints here–and–there to prepare them. We congratulated ourselves on how well they had adjusted to life in Slovakia; how they accepted with cheerful almost–indifference their parents living in two different countries.

Unfortunately, Andy couldn't stay until New Year's Day that year. He flew home at the end of December, promising to return for Pat's birthday at the beginning of April.

I saw in the New Year alone – but not lonely – from my living room, a glass of wine in hand and *Auld Lang Syne* on my lips. I wondered aloud what the coming year would bring me.

CHAPTER TWENTY-SIX

I ran into Ján as I turned off Nedbalova Street onto Laurinská Street, both of us a minute late for our meet–up at Laboratoire. We grinned at our mutual hurry to not be the late one.

The café was surprisingly quiet for that time of day. We deliberately ignored the temptation of gourmet cakes and the chocolate ice–cream station at the entrance, and took the couple of steps up to the main seating area.

After a few polite back–and–forths about who should choose where we'd sit, we mutually agreed a table down the back by a window.

We ordered our usual espresso and latte from the waiter, who looked rather bored by the lack of bustle on that blustery January day. He edged between tables, looking for any other orders, before sidling up to the counter and tapping ours into the system with a *ho hum* expression.

I was in a wonderful mood that day. I'd not been woken too early by the boys for a change, the sun was shining despite the weather, and it was always a pleasure to see Ján. I was feeling cheerily talkative, and quick to see the funny side of everything.

"How was your weekend?" I began.

"Good. I was in Dubai."

"You were in Dubai? Just like that?"

"One of my clients is opening an office in Dubai. They thought they could do the technical work on their own, or with a local technician. But they couldn't find anyone so quickly. So, they flew me out for three days."

"Well, that's quite the boring weekend."

Ján grinned.

"I really like Dubai. I was there one time before with my family, but it was interesting to see it again on my own. The cultural, I would say the social differences, between the different groups of people – the immigrants, the locals, these groups of people, I mean – it really interests me how different the conditions are. Even in business, there are no immigrants working in the offices from what I saw. Not business people, I don't mean them – I mean the people who come from the Philippines and places like this, who come to do the labour jobs that no one else wants to do. It's big money for them, so of course they come. But they don't come for office jobs. Only locals and foreigners from the richer countries have these positions. Even walking on the streets, you have this idea of Dubai being a rich city full of tall buildings and sun and resorts. There's this side, of course, but there is more than that. It's really interesting to watch people. To have the stereotype – stereotype, yes? – broken."

The waiter slid our coffees onto the table, smoothed his hands over his brown canvas apron, and disappeared out the back door for a cigarette.

"And you, how was your weekend? Have you gone ice skating yet?"

"No. I know I should. I'm a bad mother. The kids keep asking me. But I'm on my own again now that Andy's gone back to Canada. I'm a little nervous about taking both kids on my own. Pat needs too much attention. He's always up to something."

"That reminds me. I met with Štefan last night."

Štefan was one of his best friends, who was now the boys' new guitar teacher thanks to Ján. I'd given up on the violin for the moment as it was surprisingly difficult to find an English–speaking teacher who was available for private lessons after school or over the weekend. Anyway, Tom in particular was very keen to try the guitar, and Pat always agreed with anything that might be a bit of fun.

"Oh? What did he say?"

"That the kids are full of energy, but that they were good. He enjoyed the first class."

"Oh, good. I was worried he'd find them a bit too much, to be honest. Well, we did warn him in advance what they're like."

"Of course. He likes teaching children. He's a very nice guy, very kind. He is popular in the music community. When someone needs a guitar player for a performance, they call him."

"Really? I didn't know that. That's precisely the kind of teacher I want for the boys. I think music is one of those few things that become part of your core, you know? When you hear upbeat music, you feel happy, right? When you hear sad music, you feel sad. When you're feeling angry or upset or you're in a good mood, music reinforces the positive and gets rid of the negative. It's powerful stuff. And there's so much music in Bratislava – it's such a normal part of the culture here. I really want the boys to learn it naturally, and no matter what happens in life, they'll have music in their soul to fall back on. It will help them express themselves. It's one of the regrets of my life that I never learned when I was younger. We didn't have the money. I began learning the violin in Dublin, but I had to give it up when I got too busy with work and studying for my degree. Did I ever tell you I used to be a classical music critic?"

"No. When?"

"Back in my mid–twenties, in Dublin. It was such a magical time. It was after I started learning the violin. I really wanted to learn more about classical music, and I was keen to do some writing at the same time, because I'd written for some magazines and really enjoyed it. So I figured, why not combine the two? I wrote to a few classical music magazines in different parts of Europe, offering to do articles on music history, or maybe on different musicians. This one magazine in England wrote back.

"It was edited and owned by a really interesting old man, Denby Richards. He'd been a critic for most of his life, and knew practically everything there was to know about classical music. He was married to an Australian concert pianist who he said was quite well–known back in the day. So anyway, he was interested in someone covering the Irish music scene. Would I go to the National Concert Hall and do a few reviews, and see how it goes? Well, of course I said yes. I mean, I didn't actually know much about classical music at that time, and I certainly wasn't – I'm still not – technical when it comes to music. But I knew what I liked, and figured that would be enough to get started. I was so grateful that Denby saw something in me and handed me the opportunity. It was an incredibly intense learning period. I was at the concert hall practically every night, being single at the time. It was absolute bliss. I still remember sitting one night in one of the more expensive seats, looking straight down at the orchestra and thinking, *I will never forget the incredible privilege of this moment.*

"I can't say I made a great reviewer though, because you do have to have that technical knowledge. I'm rather afraid that I probably did an injustice to more than one musician whose work I didn't like. After about a year of that, I got discontented, and Denby was discontented that I was discontented. So, I ended up telling him I quit, and he was pretty mad. Well, the sub–editor jumped in and calmed us both down, which I'll forever be grateful for. Because that led to me doing interviews with the musicians instead. That was the making of me with my writing. I got to interview some incredible musicians, some of them like really, really famous in the classical music world. I even fell in love with one of them for a day, just like that, during an interview. A Russian violinist. Unfortunately, I was with my ex–boyfriend at the time, so it couldn't go anywhere, but – oh! So, anyway, to cut a very long story short – this is why I want the boys to have music as their fall–back. Something they can turn to, and express themselves through. I'm very grateful that Štefan seems to be the right type to teach them. I just hope he can handle their energy."

"Don't worry," Ján twinkled impishly. "I told him it's OK to use a wooden spoon or a belt if they're too much trouble. That's what we do here in Slovakia. It happened to me as a child. I am OK. But it didn't stop me."

"You're terrible," I giggled.

"It reminds me of something I read about the philosopher, Schopenhauer. That basically the world is an evil place. It'll never be a good place and people can't be, either, but we can do or experience certain things to lift ourselves above it – just a little."

"Sounds like he was smacked a lot as a child."

"At least he would agree with you about music. That was my point."

"So, we're all doomed, but put on some music, and somehow it'll all be OK in the meantime."

Ján shook his head at me, smiling.

In this manner, we chatted and teased for another forty–five minutes before he threw back the last of his most recent espresso.

"I'm sorry, I have to go. I must meet my sister. I'll walk with you – she lives near where you're going."

We paid our bill, slipped on our overcoats, and stepped out onto the wet cobblestones with tiny splats of snow instantly beading our faces and clothing. I loved these coffees with him. I always left feeling amused, listened to, and with something new to think about.

CHAPTER TWENTY-SEVEN

I was hard at work on a client project one night when a *déjà vu* notification appeared on my screen.

"Greetings from Rome, I am next to the Colosseum on a business trip, waiting for the check so I can go back to the hotel to sleep."

Wow, I thought. *Rome.*

"I intend to visit Bratislava to extend my business next two weeks from now. I am developing my business internationally. Belgium, Luxembourg, Bucharest so far! It would be great if you would like to meet me," Józef wrote. "I forgot Berlin," he added as an afterthought.

I was cautiously pleased to hear from him. I didn't want him out of my life altogether, but I'd made no attempt to contact him since we last spoke.

"Sure, I'd be happy to meet with you during your whirlwind business expansion tour," I replied.

"Sounds great," he wrote back immediately. "By the way, do you know of sorts of business office spaces for short term/address lending offices in Bratislava? I need a place to pay some small rent for the address and the possibility of renting a room on hourly/daily basis. If you see any, please let me know."

"For sure."

"I am on the board now. I am the one to issue invoices."

"That's a great super power."

"Isn't it?"

"I'm glad everything is going so well for you in life."

"Thank you. I hope it is so for you."

"Yes, everything is really fantastic in all parts of my life right now," I could honestly tell him.

"All? That sounds more than interesting... boyfriend?! OK, maybe I am too curious."

I wasn't sure how he jumped to that conclusion, but the tease in me wouldn't deny it.

"Enjoy Rome – I envy you so much," I replied, without acknowledging his comment. "I hope to get there one of these days."

"My curiosity will kill me," he persisted, returning to the topic, "But I am waiting till our meeting – OK."

"I'm sure you have more interesting things in your life to be curious about," I told him, smiling to myself.

"No way – you are in the very scope of my interest."

Uh huh.

"Let me know when you decide to come and I'll make sure I'm around. I'm guessing you'll have a hotel room as you are so rich now, but you're welcome to the sofa if you don't find anywhere and if your wife is OK with that. I live right near the presidential palace now, so I'm very central either way."

"Well, I didn't say I'm rich, I intend to be. I am well–to–do now not to worry about basics, that's it. I'm not coming by private plane. My check is here. Have a good night and hopefully see you in two weeks."

"Just be careful. Who knows what he'll do?" was Andy's decided opinion when I told him about the conversation. I wanted to be above–board and open with him about such things.

"I'm not an animal. I'm not going to throw myself in his arms just because he's here. Give me credit for more self–control than that."

"I don't trust him."

"Like I said. Anyway, it takes two to tango, and I'm not stupid."

"Well, you were stupid about him before, don't forget."

"That's really not very nice," I replied, miffed, despite knowing he was right. "That was ten years ago. Anyway, why do you care? We've been separated for a while now," I threw back at him crossly.

"OK, I'm sorry. I'm sorry. But I think you know I'm right about this," Andy continued.

"Well, I'm not going to lie, I'm definitely open to meeting *someone*. It would be nice to have a bit of romance in my life. To have someone remember Christmas and my birthday and Valentine's Day. And flowers! Wouldn't that be nice?," I teased, half–serious, half really not. "There's nothing wrong with that."

"No, there's not."

"I want to be loved, and to love. Why should I close myself off to potential romance?"

"Not with anyone else. I just wouldn't advise it with him."

"I didn't mean *him*; I meant more generally. But anyway, yes, back to Józef. He's here on business. Not to see me *per se*. He asked to catch up while he's here. Yes, I said he's welcome to kip on the sofa if he wants to. It was too rushed last time he was here, and anyway, I didn't have the space then. If nothing else, he's an old friend who goes back a long way. Besides, I don't even know if he's staying in Bratislava overnight. He just said he'd be here. If he does, and if he sleeps on the sofa, what better protection against anything happening if not the presence of two small kids? Not to forget, he's back with his wife. There are lines I will never cross, and that's one of them."

"Fine. Your decision."

"Thank you. I want to always be respectful of your opinion, within reason. All I can do is promise you to be careful. Come on, it's not like I'm naïve when it comes to him. And like I said, he's here on business. That's it."

I'm not sure who I was trying to convince. But Andy let it drop, and we pursued another topic.

I carried on with my life over the next two weeks, not putting much energy into thinking about Józef. I was busy with other things and anyway, from experience, he couldn't always be relied upon to follow through on what he said. If he came, he came. If he didn't, *c'est la vie*.

My relaxed attitude this time around was just as well. By 9pm the day before he was supposed to arrive, I'd still heard not a peep from him. I debated whether or not to get in touch to see if he was coming, but I'd find out either way, right? But nor did I wish to be rearranging plans at the last moment if he did turn up. So, I pondered a bit more before sending him a quick message.

"Are you in Bratislava tomorrow?"

"Yes, of course," he wrote back. "Will you be around?"

"Yes, of course. I live here," I joked. "What are your plans?

"Still under construction. I want to visit some office spaces and do some quick sightseeing. Is Ivanka airport far from the centre?"

"It's about 10km or so I think.". Then, "Are you on your own, or with your business partner?"

"On my own."

"Happy to meet up with you whenever it works for you. Are you staying overnight, or just tomorrow?"

"I will be arriving in the evening, so definitely staying overnight. I'll stay till Thursday or Friday. I have my plane back on Friday (there is no connection on Thursday), but maybe I will have to come back by train earlier."

Ah. His usual get–out–of–jail–free–card was in place, just in case.

"Where are you staying?"

"I don't know yet. Can you recommend me anything?"

"Nice to see how well–organised you are, leaving everything to the last minute!"

I thought hard for a few moments about my previous offer, before, cautiously, "You're still welcome to stay here if you like. Otherwise, I can recommend several hotels that I know of in the area."

The polite friend in me hoped he would stay; the other part really hoped he'd opt for the lesser complication of a hotel.

"Well, Bratislava is a civilised place. Thank you, however, I don't want to be a nuisance for you."

"Totally up to you. But if you prefer a hotel, that's of course OK too. Hotel Tatra, Austria Trend Hotel, and Falkensteiner Hotel are all very close to me."

"OK, I am convinced. I will gladly stay at your place. Thank you again for the invitation. Are you sure it is no problem for you?"

The more he wondered, the more my inner doubts began to surge.

"It's no problem," I declared despite my misgivings. "I don't however wish to be a potential problem with your wife, that's all. We are just friends now, of course. Andy won't be pleased, but we're separated, so I don't think he can reasonably tell me not to have guests. So basically: yes. I'm happy to have you stay and it's no problem to me personally, and it would be quite nice to spend time catching up with you. I just have those two reservations. Not sure if I'm being silly."

"OK. See you tomorrow then."

Overwhelmed with nerves and uncertainty, I called Andy. I was scared about how he would now react, but even more fearful about keeping this from him. As I dialled his number, my hands shook more than a little.

"Hey."

"Hey. What's up?"

I dove straight into it.

"Oh god. OK. So."

"What?"

"So, you know how we're separated, right?"

"Uh, yeah, I do."

"So, oh god."

"What? Jesus, woman, spit it out."

"So. Just let me finish before you say anything, OK? I don't want you hitting the roof before you've heard it all."

"*What*? Tell me!"

"Józef is going to be in town tomorrow, as I told you before."

"Yeah?"

"Remember I said he could maybe stay here?"

"OK, but..."

"No, let me finish, please," I rushed, nearly breathless as I blethered it all out. "I was going to suggest a hotel anyway, but it's only for a night, maybe two, and it's not like we're going to be doing anything. He's married, and I don't do that sort of thing. If any other close friend, male or female, was in town, I'd do the same thing, so he's not like a special exception. I couldn't be rude by saying he can't stay here without a good reason."

"You couldn't be rude... sheesh. OK. I mean, number one, you can do what you want, but number two, honestly, I don't think it's fair to his wife for him to be staying there with you," declared Andy, pursuing a different angle. "I don't think you guys would do anything, but just think how it looks. It's not something that'll ever look good when she finds out, and she *will* find out. You women always find out."

"That's true. We do find out."

"If he's there on business, he has the money to afford a hotel. He wouldn't have just assumed he'd be staying with you, even if you offered."

"You're right," I agreed, greatly relieved by his practicality. "Thank you. It's what I was telling myself deep down. I don't want to be *that* person to another woman."

"I know. Listen, I don't think you're being rude by changing your mind. Just tell him the truth, that you had second thoughts. If he's decent, he'll understand."

I was blown away by how relaxed Andy was being. I was impressed, and very proud of him.

"Thank you. I'm so glad we can be open about these things."

"Well, of course. I'm a cool dude. I can handle it. Anyway, god. I thought it was worse. I thought you were calling to say you're pregnant or something."

"Don't wish that complication upon me just yet, thank you very much."

Andy laughed.

After a couple more minutes of less–tense chit–chat, we hung up.

I messaged Józef straight back. "Second thoughts: best to book a hotel room. I just don't want to cause any issues for your wife. But book one of those hotels I mentioned, as they're near me. You're welcome to spend the evenings here chatting (and during the day when you have time) until you go back to your hotel. Is that OK with you? I'm sorry to change things, but I do want to see plenty of you while you're here, of course. Like I said, Falkensteiner and Hotel Tatra are very close."

Józef had already logged off for the evening by the time I sent my message. I had to wait nervously until morning for his response.

Which was a simple "OK. No problem."

I wasn't sure if that was a brusque or a philosophical or a nonchalant *no problem*, but it would do for now.

"When do you arrive?"

"8:25pm. I just booked Tatra."

"Great! It's about four minutes or so from me by foot. Come straight here from the airport then if you like (or check in and come straight here). I'm usually up until 1am."

"Great."

"Would you like to eat dinner with me? Or will you eat first?"

"With pleasure. However, a small one, since I am trying to control my weight."

"I will do my best! I sent you my new address already. My name is on the buzzer. So, have a good day, and I look forward to catching up with you later."

CHAPTER TWENTY-EIGHT

Pat and Tom were finally asleep, lulled into slumber by a long–winded audio story that I chose very deliberately.

I kept an eye on the time on the oven, preparing each dinner element in accordance to my guess about when Józef would most likely arrive. Forty–five minutes to get through the airport, into a taxi, to the hotel, and checked in. Ten minutes to walk to my apartment, including five or six minutes to get his bearings, miss the underpass, find the underpass, and figure out which direction to turn at the other end. One minute to be buzzed in and take the stairs up to my door.

In plopped the potatoes into the hot salty water, on went the cream sauce, in slipped the chicken into the sizzling butter. Out came the placemats, the plates, the cutlery, the glasses. Calm, orderly, precise. The very opposite of how I actually felt as the minutes flicked closer to the estimated moment of the downstairs buzzer doing its thing.

As it happened, I was only a minute or so off in my timing.

Triiing went the buzzer. I pressed the little red button to let him in.

I could hear the sound of Józef's shoes sounding uncertainly on the stone floor below, figuring out which direction to find the stairs.

I leaned over the green stairwell guardrail, and called out a *hi* to guide him along.

And then he was there in my doorway. I immediately took the lead to give him a friendly kiss on the cheek, setting the scene.

This time, everything was different. He was back with his wife and I had, for the most part, moved on from the confusion of our last encounter. I was steeled against any games that might be played.

Józef took off his black overcoat, placed it over mine on a nearby chair, and presented me with a little white gift bag.

"Something from my mother. I told her I was coming to Bratislava again, so she gave me this for you," he nodded, as I pulled out a gold star.

It was the size of my little finger tip, designed to be worn on a necklace chain.

"She told me to tell you, it's a 'star for a star'."

I was touched.

"It's adorable. Thank you. Your mother is always so kind to me," I blushed with delight. "I'll write to thank her tomorrow."

"She always liked you. Most of my other girlfriends, she didn't much like. But you were different. I don't know why."

I smiled. "Are you hungry?"

"Starving."

"Great! It's almost ready."

"Do you need any help?"

"Thank you, I'm good. I'll be done in a minute. I just have to serve."

"Can I take a quick look around?"

"Sure! The boys are asleep, they'll not hear a thing."

I steadied my nerves by plating up the meal.

Józef returned to the kitchen a couple of minutes later. "Your new place is great," he enthused. "Nothing like Leeson Street, of course…"

"Dear old Leeson Street. Not the biggest apartment in the world as you'll remember, but it was a colourful spot in those days."

"How do you sleep without the noise of nightclubs?" he joked.

"I've got two kids, and work late into the night. I'm usually out like a light whenever I fall into bed these days," I smiled back.

With everything now set on the table, we sat down to our late dinner. I served him his buttery pan–seared chicken breast with mashed potatoes, green beans, and a creamy onion sauce infused with hints of mustard and *herbs de provence*. As I didn't eat meat, I enjoyed a very realistic substitute to the chicken.

We made casual, light–hearted chit–chat as we ate. What else could one do, with a mouth full of mashed potato?

Then, after dinner ("Thank you. It was really excellent!"), we moved into the living room with its cosy low lamp light and the toasty warmth of the radiator.

Although I had absolutely sworn not to touch any wine around him this time, given the *in vino veritas* nature of my tongue, the awkwardness seemed a hell of a lot easier to overcome with a steadying glass in front of me. I had got Józef some *Staropramen* beer, which he much preferred over wine.

We slowly sipped away at our drinks, hovering at first around those ultra–reliable conversational stalwarts of work and parents and hobbies. He explained the business he hoped to do in Bratislava, and sounded me out about whether I'd be interested in potentially working with him and his business partner.

Eventually, as the alcohol began to relax and loosen, we inevitably began to probe each other about the current status of our respective love lives.

For me, nothing much had really changed. Andy and I were still on our unhurried meander towards divorce. There was no animosity, no uncertainty between us. The path was clear.

As for Józef, he and his wife appeared to get along perfectly well now, from what I gathered from his few brief comments as the night wore on. Aside, that is, from mysterious hints at familial pressures of one type or another, which I understood to mean her parents. I didn't suppose him madly in love, as that had never been his style. But he had nothing bad to say about her, so I could safely assume he cared for her as deeply as he wished. All the same, I got the sense he was keeping much to himself. I knew it would be fruitless to probe for what he didn't want to share, and it was not in my nature to wish someone else unhappy for the sake of my bruised ego.

I snuck a quick peek at Józef's face as he glanced down at his beer. Although his hair was perhaps a little thinner than it used to be, and he somehow seemed worldlier behind that neutral façade, his face was still as smooth and unbothered as it had ever been.

Józef looked up at me. I smiled quickly to deflect the fact I'd been staring.

"You know, you look really well," he told me.

"What, despite you telling me last time that I'm fatter than I used to be?"

"No, me? I would never say that."

"Mmm hmm."

"Well, this time I think you could safely put on one or two kilos."

"Gee, thank you."

I swallowed a sip of wine the wrong way as I gave a little laugh. I spluttered inelegantly, wet mascara pricking the corners of my eyes as tears appeared.

"Are you OK?"

"I think so," I replied, once I'd caught my breath. "I'm used to you making me cry, don't you know."

He laughed, playfully reached for my hand, and kept a hold of it casually while we talked. His fingers were long and warm, and tremendously smooth.

I couldn't recall noticing that about him before. Probably because he'd never been a hand–holder in the past, I supposed. I leveraged the observation to spin the moment into a light–hearted one, protecting myself from attaching any sense of impropriety or meaningfulness to his gesture.

"These are the hands of a pianist, or of someone who doesn't get much involved with the dish–washing, I'll take it? Seriously, how do you have such smooth hands?"

"Really, they're so smooth? It must be a gift of the gods," he mused.

I pulled my hand away gently.

"That must be it."

He took my hand back, more serious this time.

"I'm sorry if I hurt you in the past somehow. It was never my intention."

I blushed, pulled my hand away again, and nodded. I was not tipsy enough to brush it off, or sober enough to discuss it. But I deeply appreciated the apology.

"Anyway, I suppose I should go. It's getting late."

He was right; it was after midnight already, just like that.

At the door, I gave him a deliberately casual hug and a kiss on the cheek.

"Hopefully we'll see each other tomorrow," he told me. "It's possible I might have to get a train back home for an urgent meeting. I'll know around midday."

The next morning as I concentrated on my work, my phone rang beside the lap–top. I'd been so absorbed in what I was doing, that the sound made me jump.

"So, good news. I don't have to go to that meeting. I am here for another day."

"Great!"

"I've just finished my second appointment. We can go for lunch if you like. I'm very near."

"I've just got to finish a quick project for a client. Why don't you come around here and have a cup of tea, then we'll head out and do lunch and a bit of sightseeing."

Five minutes later, the buzzer went off. I let him in downstairs, and left open my front door as I ran back to the lap–top to quickly finish up.

Józef made himself a cup of *Melissa* tea from the pack I'd picked up for him, remembering it was his favourite kind.

Within a few minutes, I'd finished and proofread the document, and sent it off to my client.

"Sorry about the wait. We can go. What would you like to see?"

"Maybe the old town? The castle seems like a good place to start."

"Alright. Sounds like a plan."

The late January afternoon was chillier than the day before. Our coats were buttoned and zipped up tightly, and gloved hands were firmly dug into pockets. It was fresh rather than bitter though; the winter had been pleasingly mild so far.

I took him on a slightly circuitous route through Michalská brána, so that he could see a little of the historic part of old town. I then guided him through some quieter laneways until we reached Most SNP.

We walked under the bridge and then climbed the stone stairway up to the castle. Despite playing basketball and tennis, Józef was not used to walking further than his car or around a supermarket. I couldn't help but giggle at his attempts to conceal his huffing and puffing as we made our way up.

"You are laughing at me."

"Of course. Who wouldn't?"

"It's my new shoes."

"Oh, I'm sure. Well, we can walk slower to accommodate your poor shoes."

At the ramparts, we stopped to take in the view. He didn't seem particularly interested in any one thing, so I pointed out the wind turbines that marked the Austrian border, the thoroughly unbeautiful yet eye–catching functionalist concrete high–rise housing units of Petržalka, and the rapidly–changing skyline all around us dotted with cranes and new buildings. We debated what the statue of the mounted Svätopluk was looking at in the far distance. Then we quickly walked through the castle courtyard, skirting the groups of Japanese tourists and local schoolchildren before heading back down in the general direction of old town and the Museum of Clocks.

I was so busy chatting away, keeping up a more–or–less one–side conversation, that I didn't notice we had almost literally hit a stone wall.

"Hmm, I thought it was here."

"What?"

"The exit. I was distracted. That's what happens when you're not paying attention."

"You don't know the way out?"

"Well no, it seems not, but I'm sure we'll find it soon enough," I smiled.

"You shouldn't have told me that. You could have pretended you knew," he admonished, trying to make light of the situation.

I laughed at his unwarranted seriousness. "It's not rocket science. We're up, old town is down."

"But here is a wall."

I smiled at the irony. "Oh, come on. Live a little. If you hit walls in life, you look around until you find a door, right? Or, in this case..." I trailed off, as I stepped quickly ahead to investigate a promising hint further down the path, before coming back to fetch him, "an old passageway. Let's see where it takes us. You wanted a tour, didn't you?"

Józef half–smiled away his uncertainty, and followed me.

I had, in fact, discovered a very smart shortcut that took us almost directly down to the bottom of the hill.

"See? I told you!" I grinned triumphantly.

Józef gave a small smile back, graciously allowing me the victory.

"So? Where to for coffee?" he asked, changing topic.

"Follow me. If you dare, of course!" I shot back at him.

I took him to Laboratoire on Laurinská, a place that surely couldn't fail to please. We took a seat towards the middle, placing our coats on one of the empty chairs by our table.

"I feel like I'm cheating on Ján, somehow," I admitted lightly as we beckoned over the waiter.

Józef raised an eyebrow. "Why?"

"The only other time I came here was with him. It's usually either him or Michaela that I meet up with. So it seems kind of weird to be coming to a café with someone else."

"Oh? How often do you meet with this guy?"

"Fairly often, I'd say. We're meeting up tomorrow, in fact," I winked.

"I see. That's nice."

"Isn't it?" I grinned back, rather naughtily.

Józef didn't know what to say, so he let it drop.

Despite the watching of his waistline, even Józef found the temptations of Laboratoire's chocolate delights too strong to resist. I had a latte and a croissant, and Józef an organic milk chocolate pot. His silky treat soon arrived, all €4.50 and 100mls or so of it, artfully stacked with chopped strawberries and accompanied by the most heavenly chocolate scent. His exhale of pleasure at the last spoonful was a review enough.

We didn't stay long. Józef needed to rest after our walk, and I had to pick up the boys from school. I would see him again later on, as he promised to come around for dinner that night as well.

CHAPTER TWENTY-NINE

I was tremendously nervous all afternoon after Józef and I parted. This time, he would be around early enough in the evening to meet my children. There was something complicatedly nerve-wracking about the notion: partially the sense of introducing him to my physical connection to another man, and partially the fear of Pat and Tom becoming too friendly – or not – with someone they may never see again, but who had played such a convoluted role in my life.

A few minutes before he was due to appear, my phone rang.

"Hi, it's me."

I immediately assumed what he was going to tell me. He was going to run away after all. I was furiously disappointed, mostly at myself for beginning to trust him. I should have known better. No, I *did* know better.

"Hi," I replied, deliberately casual.

"So, I have an unexpected problem. I need to go to the train station."

I knew it.

"Oh? I'm sorry to hear that."

"The guys at the hotel are trying to help me. It seems that when I went to check in for my flight online, my return date is actually in one month. As much as I'd like to stay for a month, I need to be back home tomorrow, and I fly to Dubai on Sunday for holiday. The hotel guys said I need to book a train directly at the station. It can't be done online, somehow. I'm sorry, I'll be thirty or forty-five minutes late. But I'll be there."

"No problem, we'll see you when you're done," I replied, cautiously pleased.

Within the hour, just as he'd said, he was at the door, bottle of wine in hand.

Tom and Pat, forever excited by who the doorbell might bring, dashed out into the hall to greet him.

"Hi!" called Tom.

"Who is this guy?" Pat asked.

"I'm Józef. You must be...?"

"Pat."

"I knew that. You're Pat, that's Tom."

"That's right!" Tom agreed.

"Are you a friend of Mummy's?" Pat asked.

"Yes. For a long time."

"I love this guy!" Pat enthused, looking up at me.

"Thank you. I like you very much, too." Józef grinned down at him.

For all his aura of emotional practicality, Józef was thoroughly at ease around little ones. He gravitated towards babies and toddlers in particular with almost grandfatherly delight.

Tom and Pat picked up on this immediately. Józef was soon being drawn into interrogations about his life by Pat, and shown how to play games on the tablet as Tom directed Józef's efforts from his lap.

I found it all extremely surreal.

The million loud questions continued over dinner as I served and ensured that everyone was fed, while stopping every five seconds to tell Pat to get back in his chair, stop playing with his food, and for goodness' sake go to the toilet instead of making that face.

Afterwards, Józef relaxed in the pleasant low–light of the sitting room while I got the kids cleaned up, dressed for bed, read to, watered, kissed, and off to sleep.

When the boys were finally quiet, and the kitchen was tidied up, I joined Józef in the living room with the bottle of wine, two glasses, and a bottle opener.

"I'm impressed," he told me immediately, as he opened and poured the wine. "You're rather strict with them at the dinner table, but I can see they are well–behaved and are good boys."

"Thank you," I replied, taking the glass from his outstretched hand.

We clinked glasses, and took a sip.

"They have a great life here. They really do. Bratislava is incredible. Nothing compared to your city, of *course*..."

"Of course."

"... but I love it. The boys have a wonderful school. I've made some great friends. We eat well. There's just so much to do. And glorious Vienna is just over the border."

"How is work? Are you earning enough to afford everything?"

"More or less. Some months it's harder, especially when Andy has a slow month, too. I don't like to rely on him when he has his own debts and expenses to worry about. It makes me feel bad to ask him to help more. But I've got to the point now where I'm just telling myself, that I have to find a way to make sure that I'm earning enough to cover everything. Then I don't need to worry about relying on anyone for anything."

"If you ever need it, I can lend you something."

I blushed at his offer, embarrassed and touched. "Thank you so much. I'm very grateful."

He smiled, and nodded, and dropped the subject with a "Just so you know."

"And, um, what time is your train tomorrow? Did you get it sorted?"

"Yes. Eleven ten. Unfortunately – or maybe fortunately – I had to buy first–class tickets. The woman at the counter said second–class was fully booked. I will travel in style."

"How long is the trip?"

"Seven hours. I was wondering, perhaps you could loan me a book?"

"Of course. I'll take a look at what I have, and you can choose."

We chatted easily for another hour or more, mostly reminiscing.

After a half–bottle of wine, he reached out again and held my hand like he had the evening before. "Come, embrace me for a moment."

He pulled me towards him, an arm around my shoulder, a certain look upon his face.

I rested against his chest for the briefest of moments before pulling away sharply – reluctantly – from the nostalgic warmth of his scent.

"I can't, it's not right. How would she feel if she knew?"

"It's just an embrace. Nothing more."

I shook my head, more frustrated with myself than him.

"Can I tell you, you're just like a big ship," I blurted out.

"A big ship?"

"Yes. You're like this big ship, which doesn't see the little ships because you're too focused on getting out of the harbour first. I don't want to use the word 'selfish', because I don't think that's precisely it. But you're so focused on your own goals, your own needs, that your big ship knocks the rest of us out of your way."

Józef was silent.

"I'm sorry. I don't mean to offend. That's just how I visualise the way you have always treated me."

He still didn't say a word, aside from a quiet *hmm*. He kept a hold of my hand, however, weaving his fingers between mine as he thought.

Then, out of nowhere, he exclaimed, "It's just that I don't want to end up having three kids with three different women."

I felt a thrill of agonised longing as those words sunk in. The me of ten years ago and the me of now were very different women, however. This would not do.

I looked around, keen to break the moment. "Would you like some more wine?"

"Sure."

"Well, we've run out. Would you mind running across the road and grabbing some?"

"Oh, come on. You know I don't walk that far."

"It's literally across the road. You have long legs. I'm sure you can manage it."

He got up reluctantly, yet amused all the same.

"You're not kicking me out?"

"Of course not. The night is still young. But wine–less. Go on, the fresh air will do you good. I'll pay for this one."

Józef refused. "It's my pleasure."

"Thank you so much. I really appreciate that."

He was back within ten minutes with a new bottle of the same wine. He poured me a glass, and himself a glass, and settled back into the sofa.

Finally stripped of the blinkered nostalgia of yesteryear, I was beginning to see Józef in a very different, more thoughtful light. This was no great love story, merely two people with very different ideals about love and relationships. Despite knowing so much of each other, we knew very little *about* each other. What his heart wanted was as unfathomable to me as what he could comprehend about mine. His guard was always raised, even despite the alcohol. It made it difficult to be fully comfortable in his presence. It had always been that way, but now, my happiness wasn't tied up with it. It was a self–revelation that both grieved and freed me.

At midnight, Józef put on his coat, slipped on his shoes, and thanked me for the evening.

"Thank you, too. I'll take you to the train station tomorrow, if you like," I offered.

"I like the idea very much, if you have the time," he replied.

"Sure, happy to. I've got to take the kids to school and go to the gym, but I can meet you around ten. I have coffee with Ján at eleven–thirty, but I can fit you in for sure."

"Ah, Ján. Your coffee friend."

"Yes."

"You really like meeting him for coffee?"

"Yes. He's kind, and he's thoughtful, and he's interesting and sincere, and I've known him a long time, and we have great conversations. He doesn't mess me around. What's not to like? Also, he enjoys coffee, unlike yourself," I added mischievously.

"I don't want to interfere with your plans."

"It's fine. I can do both. Where shall we meet?"

"My hotel room? I'm in room 415. Wake me in case I sleep in. I don't want to miss my train. Would you do that for me?"

"Of course." I kissed his cheek and gave a little wave as the sound of his thick shoes reverberated down the stone steps in the late evening hush of the building.

CHAPTER THIRTY

The following morning after school and the gym, I quickly ran over to Michalská brána to pick up an additional something for Józef's mother. I wanted to give her something practical and useful, pretty and memorable. After some debate, I eventually decided on a hand–painted art nouveau–style tea light. I then sent Józef a message to check if he was up yet.

He had just finished breakfast and was packing his bag, but told me to come over and meet him.

I replied to let him know that I'd be there in a few minutes, and began walking to his hotel.

The Tatra Hotel aimed for a polished and moneyed look in the foyer, yet retained something of communist functionalism in its appearance and scent. I found it quite fascinating.

I took a slow lift up to the fourth floor. It binged and I stepped out, just in time to catch Józef walking towards the other lifts in the opposite direction.

He turned back as I called out, explaining that he'd been about to meet me downstairs. Józef guided me to his room, where he immediately threw himself back down on the bed for a few minutes to rest his hungover head.

I gave him a choice of books for his journey. We alternated between idle chit–chat and silence while he chose one.

After Józef had checked out, I beckoned him towards the underpass by the presidential palace. He walked slowly in his new shoes, or because he wasn't used to walking, or because he was hungover.

Whatever the reason, I good–humouredly regulated my usual brisk pace to match his.

Once in the underpass, we turned left, walked down the stairs, up the escalators, and came up on the Poštová side outside the Panta Rhei bookstore.

I'd observed the uncertainty on his face a good minute or so before he finally said something.

"Where are you taking me?"

"To the Number 1 tram," I replied.

"I got the bus to the station yesterday. It was in the opposite direction."

"The Number 1 goes there, too."

"The bus wasn't in this direction."

"You don't trust me?"

"It's not that I don't trust you. It's just that I'm not sure this is the right direction."

"I live here, you know. I know which direction the station is," I declared, bemused.

Józef didn't say anything else for a few moments, but the same look shaded his face until we reached the tram stop on Obchodná.

"See?" I pointed out, tapping at the timetable more than a little gleefully. "Hlavná stanica. The main train station. The tram will be here in three minutes, and you'll still have twenty minutes when we get there before your train leaves."

He tipped his head to one side in acknowledgement.

"You're welcome to find your own way to the station next time though," I smiled.

Józef shook his head at me.

"Are you still planning on coming back in a month?" I casually enquired.

"Well, unless something urgent comes up, I think so. It was an expensive ticket, so I had rather buy a one–way here to use the return part of my current ticket, than waste it completely. I might have some business here by then."

I nodded.

"Would you like that?" he asked, looking down into my eyes.

I glanced up at him.

"Would you like to see me again?"

I didn't know what to say. So, I just smiled a brief smile, and hoped that it conveyed all the nuances of what I couldn't express.

Józef didn't press me any further.

The Number 1 tram pulled up, and we hopped on. A mere eight minutes later, the correct tram had taken us in the correct direction to the correct station.

We stopped at a kiosk inside the concourse so Józef could buy something to drink for the train.

I looked around until I spotted his platform number. I guided him through the throng to the crisp breeze of the outdoor platform on the other side of the hall. We found an uncrowded spot where we estimated the first–class carriage would be.

"Are you sure this is the right platform?" he asked.

"What do you mean?"

"Are you sure this is Platform One? Track and platform can be different things, can they not?"

"Are you serious? I think for the purposes, they're one and the same. And yes, this is Platform One. It's written above the entrance to the platform."

"OK, if you're sure."

"Yep, I'm sure. But if you'd like to go and double–check, you're welcome to do so."

"No, it's OK, I trust you."

But, less than ten seconds later: "Maybe it's a good idea to check anyway. I trust you, but I don't want to miss my train.".

Józef left me with his suitcase as he walked back inside to the concourse. I was frustrated and amused; mostly the former. I was even beginning to doubt myself now.

He returned a minute later, a diplomatic smile on his lips. "It seems this is Platform One."

At that very moment, the details of the coming train flashed up on the screen, accompanied by a not–to–be–doubted announcement. "The eleven–ten EuroCity to Warsaw via Budapest and Bratislava is now arriving on Platform One."

As if to remove any lingering doubts, the train glided in quickly, before coming to a halt precisely where it should.

I walked with Józef to his carriage door.

"Thank you for everything," he told me.

"You're very welcome. It was great to see you." I gave him a friendly kiss on the cheek and a brief hug. In former times, I cared very much about our goodbyes. But I simply couldn't do it again. I spun around and walked directly through the concourse and out to the tram stop on the other side to meet up with Ján in town.

I didn't look back.

CHAPTER THIRTY-ONE

On a Monday morning towards the end of February, I quickly scanned the news headlines online while the kids were getting dressed for school. I'd had about three hours' sleep the night before due to a client project, so I was desperate for some coffee along the way.

Investigative journalist killed in his house: The Interior Ministry confirmed on the morning of February 26 that the investigative journalist of the Aktuality.sk website, Ján Kuciak, was found dead in his house, obviously murdered

screamed the main headline in *The Slovak Spectator*.

I was astonished. Surely this couldn't happen in a small country like Slovakia? I read on with disbelief.

The details were sparse at this stage, but the newspaper could at least share that Kuciak and his fiancé Martina Kušnírová were found dead in their home, shot and left dead for up to four days before their bodies were discovered. It was immediately suspected that they'd been killed because of Kuciak's work, possibly linked to his current investigation into the suspected theft of EU funds by Italian mafia based in eastern Slovakia. It was all so unbelievable. How could this happen *here*? I felt so sorry for the couple and their families. I hoped they'd catch the killer quickly.

By the following day there were dozens of candles, both lit and windblown, paying homage to a large photograph of Ján and Martina against the wall of Kostol Navštívenia Panny Márie on Námestie SNP.

Pat and Tom were extremely curious. Why were so many people gathered around the wall, whispering and shaking their heads? Why were there so many candles that weren't there yesterday? Who were the guy and girl in the picture?

It was one of the most difficult parenting decisions I'd ever had to make, and I had to make it immediately, and on my own. I could have shielded them from the truth, but we passed by this spot every day and no doubt the kids at school would talk. So, I told them what had happened, not in graphic detail of course, but there was enough talk of bad guys and guns and naughty politicians to ensure that they understood the basics.

Andy was fully supportive of me telling them the truth.

"You're right, it's important," he agreed wholeheartedly during one of our evening chats. "It's not like you can avoid them seeing the candles and everything. They're old enough now to know something of it. They have to learn about death some day, right? And like you said, this is big there. It's a huge history lesson."

Over the coming days, graphic posters and handwritten signs appeared alongside the candles, including a t–shirt with a hole and painted splatters of blood, a miniature coffin lid, and several pictures of the murdered couple and certain politicians. The air was tense with anticipation.

Now the boys could talk of little else on the way to and from school but guns and murder, constantly comparing their sweetly childish ideas on how they'd deal with the bad guys.

"It's horrible. They were so young, just twenty–seven. They were going to get married in May, you know." Michaela shook her head and stared down into her soup when we met up for lunch at Thali on the Wednesday.

"There's a photo of them on SNP Square, where all the candles are, have you seen it? They look so in love in that picture. It's just awful, one minute they're pottering around their house just doing their thing, the next these thugs break into their home and end their lives for purely selfish reasons. It's just so unfair," I sighed.

"Are you going to the protest about it on Friday?" she asked.

"I'm thinking yes."

"Things might get ugly," Michaela foretold gloomily. "Everyone's really angry with the government about what's happening. No one expected this. It takes everything to a whole new level."

"Did you see the news story about the Prime Minister, the Interior Minister, and the Police Chief with the one million euro on the table, offering it as a reward to anyone who comes forward with information about the murder?"

"Yes," she replied indignantly. "Straight out of a bad Hollywood movie. Well, we'll have to see what happens after this Friday. There are protests all around the country too, did you hear? Also in some foreign cities. The government should listen."

Going home with the boys later that afternoon, we were handed printed flyers advertising the protest. The lady giving them out told me eagerly in English that children were welcome, and that they expected a child–friendly zone to be set up outside Stará tržnica. It sounded like it was expected to be a large–scale gathering.

"You're going?" asked Oskar with a wave, as the boys and I walked past the Pán Králiček wagon. He had seen the flyer in my hands.

I stopped. "Yes, I think so. I really want to. We live here, and I want us to stay here, so it's important to show our support."

"Thank you for supporting our country," Oskar enthused. "Really, it's so nice of you. It's important to us, too. We're *not* sheep."

The next day, I met up with Ján at Kaviareň Houm for coffee ("This used to be something else... can't remember what the name was. I came here with my sister once. It's definitely more hipster now.").

It was just after 11 o'clock, yet it was still relatively quiet. The server was slow to take our orders, but made up for it with the speed in which she delivered them.

I put my handbag and coat on the chair between us. My head was full of Ján Kuciak and Martina Kušnírová, which was becoming a bigger news story by the day. It had even reached the international news sites I read daily: *BBC*, *The Independent*, *The Guardian*, and several others. None of my friends abroad mixed up Slovakia and Slovenia now.

I longed to hear Ján's opinion as both someone who spoke Slovak and who was politically–aware. Translated articles were one thing; hearing the finer details from locals entirely another.

"Did you hear about the murdered journalist?" I asked pointlessly, breathless with curiosity.

"Yes, of course."

"We walk past the memorial every day. So many candles – more and more all the time."

"It's a big story in Slovakia," he replied.

"I wish I could understand more about it. I'm restricted to whatever's published in English. Actually, I have a new–found respect for *The Slovak Spectator*. I used to think their English language stories were OK but not exactly cutting–edge stuff. Now, I'm glued to it. The only thing is, as far as I can tell anyway, most of the news reports are about Ján Kuciak. I get that he's more well–known, but *she* lost her life, too. That's equally tragic. But I don't see much about her in the news."

"That's not quite true," Ján countered, putting down his espresso. "Maybe it's not reported so much, but I saw a news report where they talked for many minutes with her friends and colleagues and they discussed her life and personality."

"That's good to hear," I backed down. "It's just so tragic. It's hard to believe that something like this could happen in a place like Slovakia."

"It will be interesting to see what happens now," he responded. "They're asking for an independent investigation of the murder, and people want the interior minister to resign. The Prime Minister, Fico, says he won't resign and he doesn't agree that his ministers should resign. People also want him to remove Mária Trošková – she was a model, now she is a Fico assistant. The problem is that she is connected to people that are suspected of these murders."

"It's all incredibly shady," I grimaced. "There's a protest being organised for tomorrow on SNP Square. Will you go?"

"Yes, I think so."

"I think I'll take the kids for a bit. Anyway, it's on our way home from school. Michaela's worried about it being unsafe for the boys, because no one knows what the atmosphere will be like. I'll play it by ear and see what happens. I'd like to take them because I think it's important for us to show our support. I also want the boys to remember this – well, probably Tom more than Pat because of their ages. These events don't happen every day, and this is a critical time in Slovakia's history. I mean, when was the last time people took to the streets?"

"1989. It's when the communist government fell."

"Exactly. So, I want the boys to experience this. I feel kind of sad that I've had to explain death and real–life bad guys to them so early in life. But it's impossible to avoid when you're passing the signs and candles and that picture of the two of them every day."

Ján nodded.

"On another subject," I suddenly exclaimed as it popped into my head, "what's up with this Easter Monday tradition with women?"

"You mean the whipping?" Ján enquired, immediately enthused.

"Yes. One of my students was talking about it. I don't get it. So, basically, it's Easter Monday, and all the men in Slovakia get to go around whipping or throwing water over women to wish them health and fertility for the coming year?"

"Of course. When I was a boy, I enjoyed going to all the women in my building with my whip. An old man above us showed me how to make them. It's a great tradition!"

"You're a bunch of barbarians," I grinned, half-appalled, half-amused. "I hope no one comes after me with a whip, or I'll smack them over the head with it!"

"You should not answer your door on Easter Monday, then," he warned gleefully.

As I was hungry and Houm didn't serve much food, Ján recommended Bistro St. Germain, a very short walk away. I found it tremendously charming, with its Parisian bistro seating, the book shelves against the wall, 1930s–style floor tiles, the French–inspired menu. Ján always knew the best places to go.

I tucked into my creamy goat's cheese, pink pepper, and chive dish in a little mason jar, served with crispy baguette slices on the side. It was all so fresh and so absolutely delicious.

"How's work going? Any trips to Dubai planned again soon?"

"Maybe. They will install a new server in the Dubai office. I may have to go over, or maybe they'll find someone locally. I'll know in a few weeks."

"At least it makes life interesting, not knowing when or if you'll be jetting off to some exotic location or other for your work," I smiled, digging my fork further into the jar.

He looked at me with sudden seriousness. "It's something I've been thinking a lot about recently: should I get a full–time job, or try to find more work with the clients I have? One day when I have kids, I think it's better to have more money."

My heart sank upon hearing these words. I wondered if he was subtly warning me that these meetings wouldn't last forever. Just as I'd come to accept these get–togethers as an important fixture in my life, I became aware that one day they would of course come to an end.

And *that* is the moment I was struck by a certain dawning realisation.

As February rolled into March, the tragedy of Ján Kuciak and Martina Kušnírova began to take an increasingly ugly political turn. The Culture Minister had resigned a day after the news of their deaths had broken, professing shock at what had happened to a journalist under his watch. All seven suspects arrested over the murders were released on the day of Kuciak's funeral due to lack of evidence. The obstinate, uncertain, obfuscating behaviour of the authorities was fuelling demands for the resignation of certain key players in government.

However, if the intention had been to silence Ján Kuciak, the perpetrators had brought about quite the opposite. An international coalition of journalists formed a partnership to continue Kuciak's investigations. His final unfinished article outlining the mafia activity in eastern Slovakia was published to public uproar. Regular mass demonstrations took place in the spring cold of Námestie SNP, with people increasingly frustrated by the lack of progress in the murder investigation and their demands for change.

Things were made worse by the news of earlier threats against Kuciak having been ignored by the police, and the stubborn refusal of the Prime Minister, Interior Minister, and Police Chief to resign.

25,000 people turned out in Bratislava on the second of March. Nearly 50 other towns and cities across Slovakia, and 17 abroad, attracted protesters. Several universities cancelled classes in the afternoon to enable their students to attend. Every day, flowers and candles and tokens of commemoration and anger built up against the wall outside Kostol Navštívenia Panny Márie, forming a tidal wave that spread out ever–further into the square. It became part of the landscape, and a topic of frequent conversation for Pat and Tom.

Two weeks into the crisis, the Interior Minister finally gave in to demands and reluctantly resigned following a turnout of 50,000 people the previous Friday. The Prime Minister clutched on to power a little longer, before being manoeuvred into resignation by his coalition partners after they withdrew their support when he refused to step down. He resisted giving up his chairmanship of the party, however, sparking further public disgust.

The energy on the streets was incredible. People were becoming much more politically–aware and demanding, and talked openly about developments without fear of repercussion. The demonstrations continued almost every week, pummelling the authorities by their determination and refusal to go backwards.

"I told you, they made the mistake of thinking we're sheep," Oskar declared as he prepared my latte the day after the Prime Minister's resignation. "Have you been going to the protests?"

"Yes," I replied, as I took the cup and paid for my coffee. "We went to the first two for fifteen or twenty minutes. The boys couldn't understand anything and got too restless, so I had to take them home. I might find someone to watch them for the next one, though, so I can stay longer. I was so impressed by how calm and determined the crowds were each time."

"Perhaps we've been passive, but we didn't have a reason to be anything else these thirty years," Oskar explained. "Now that we have a good reason, we're fighting back."

CHAPTER THIRTY-TWO

Just when I had pretty much given up on hearing anything from the alien police, Timotej got in touch.

"Good news. I have your new permits," he informed me, voice brimming with success. "I even managed to get them to extend the dates to the expiry date of your new contract. Normally it's only to the end of the first contract, even if you move. It would usually be extended only when you reapply."

"Oh my god, that's incredible news," I exclaimed. "Thank you so much!"

"I have an appointment near your home this afternoon. Would you like me to drop the permits off to you?"

I gleefully agreed. I almost couldn't believe it. Finally, after ten months of hassle and drama and blood–curdling frustration, we all had our permits – with correct information. We would be free and clear for at least another year.

"Now... actually. *One* slight problem," Timotej added.

"Oh?"

"We have all permits with your new address, but Tom's still says the twenty–eighth of April instead of February next year like for you and your other son. It's not a big problem; on Tom's actual file with the police the date is now the same as yours, don't worry. The file is the official record, not the card. I will push them to reissue the card with the new date, but for now, at least he has a valid permit."

I could only shake my head. Of course, there had to be yet another problem.

True to his word, Timotej stopped by a couple of hours later and handed over the cards.

"Thank you. I am very, very impressed with your skills and service. You're amazing," I gushed. "It's been such a difference compared to the service I received from the other guy. I'll most definitely be recommending you."

"It's always great to receive positive feedback, as I'm living in the negative world of state authorities," Timotej quipped. "I'm sorry about the date on the card, but that's much easier to fix than the file."

He shook my hand, wished me and the boys very well, jumped back into his car, and drove off.

To celebrate our 95% victory, I called Michaela to join me for a quick coffee at Martinus on Obchodná before I had to get the boys from school. I was bursting with delight.

Michaela hurried through the door late as usual, spotted me by the downstairs window, and beelined her way over with a troubled look upon her face.

"Congratulations! Didn't I tell you he's far better than that other lawyer you were using?" she exclaimed, giving me a hug. "Anyway, sorry I'm late. I've got a good excuse this time. I got delayed by one of those women who are always asking for change."

"I saw a group of them on my way in here. They didn't stop me, though."

"Well, one of them stopped *me*. She approached for directions and then complimented me for talking to her, even though she's a gypsy... her words, not mine. I didn't want to be rude after she said that, so I kept talking to her. Yeah, I know. Then she asked me to show her my hand. She told me she sees death, and did I want her to prevent it from happening to me? So, I gave her my hand, and she asked me if I'd give her a hundred euro without regretting it."

"What! Oh my. At least she got straight to the point. And then what happened?"

"Well... I told her that I could only give her what's in my wallet. She offered to walk me to the ATM to get more, but I said I didn't think there's much in my account – which is true, by the way – so she took what I had in my wallet instead. Five or ten euro, I think."

"And then what?"

"She got one of my hairs and wrapped it in a tissue and muttered something into it, I don't know what. She gave me directions for what to do with it at home."

"You didn't believe her, surely?" I grinned, incredulous.

Michaela shrugged her shoulders, apprehensive.

"You just never know if they're real or not. I'm really superstitious; I believe in all that stuff. I don't want to risk it. But I'm not telling George, so definitely don't mention it to him. And *please* don't bring this up to me again. I'm careful about these things, as weird as it might seem," she shuddered.

"Don't worry. If I ever write a book about my experiences here, I'll be sure to include it. Otherwise, I promise never to mention it again."

"Thank you. Ugh, I'm shaking. Where's my *lungo*?"

"Yes, good idea, let's change subject. I just saw an ambulance driver smoking in the front seat of the ambulance. Gross."

"What's wrong with that?" Michaela wondered.

"What do you mean? That'd be a social media shitstorm in Canada," I gasped.

"Was anyone else in the ambulance at the time?"

"No."

"He wasn't hurting anyone. It's just a bit of smoke. Ambulances have windows."

My eyebrows shot up at the cultural contrast.

"Look, there's the Pink Lady!" she exclaimed suddenly, pointing out a sweet–faced old woman dressed head–to–toe in that shade at a nearby table.

She was reading a newspaper with great attention, oblivious to our stares.

"The Pink Lady's well–known in Bratislava. You know the weather's improving when she appears."

We stared at her in silence for a few moments, before moving on to another topic.

"Are you going to the latest protest this Thursday? I enquired.

"Yes. You?"

"Yes, absolutely."

"Thank you. It's still really important for us to have our voices heard."

"I agree. And why don't we make a night of it? Andy's here anyway, remember, so he can watch the kids while we go out. We could go to the protest and then have dinner somewhere afterwards. What do you think?"

"I'm in."

We met outside the presidential palace that Thursday just before 5pm, and made the short walk through the underpass to Námestie SNP, where the protest was to be held.

Tens of thousands of people surged forward from every side street, tram, bus, and shop almost at once, each making their way to the very same spot.

As with the other protests I'd been to, albeit briefly, this one radiated a very determined calm.

Michaela and I found an excellent vantage point right next to the candlelit memorial for Martina and Ján, our view only impeded by a handful of television trucks and their growling generators.

One of the reporters, a young woman with a bored expression and a lot of make–up, only became animated when the cameras were on. In between, she amused herself by flirting half–heartedly with one of the technicians as he sat in the truck, a window half–rolled down to let out the smoke from his cigarette.

The protest organisers and invited speakers appeared on stage, each taking turns to give fervent addresses. Michaela whispered regular translated summaries of what was being said so that I could follow what was happening. The speeches were interspersed with music: the national anthem, then another speech, then more music.

This time, the protest was to demand the resignation of the Police Chief, who continued to hang on to power despite even the President's calls for him to step down. The speakers – a group comprised of students and actors and social commentators – also decried governmental corruption and ineffectiveness in general. A photojournalist who had worked in the east of Slovakia took to the stage to share his on–the–ground insights.

I wouldn't describe the atmosphere as festive, but it certainly wasn't dull. The guy behind me even managed to take a moment away from his intense focus on the speeches to squeeze my bottom, before merging into the concealing mass.

Michaela and I stood for over an hour in that biting breeze. Although I couldn't understand more than a few words, I wasn't bored for a second. At the end came the ringing out of keys, a custom dating back to the final days of the communist era when people jingled their keys *en masse* to demand change.

It was all incredibly moving. I witnessed not one act of violence or anger, merely intelligence and respect. Aside from the bum pinch, that is.

Attending that protest underscored in my mind my determination to make Slovakia our permanent home if we could manage it. Aside from the greater freedom and opportunities the boys and I had here, the protests had given me unquestionable insight into the decency and vitality of the Slovak people.

As the crowd began to disperse, buzzing with energy and excitement, Michaela and I slowly made our way down to Laurinská Street for coffee at Urban House before walking over to Laboratoire for a light dinner. We'd intended to check out a jazz performance at the Bukowski Bar, but by the time we got there, the cavern–like room where the concert was being held was packed to the door. We weren't the only ones making a night of it after the protest, it seemed.

Michaela with her emerald green dress and glossy chestnut hair attracted the stares of quite a few men, including a cheerful drunk at the bar. She blithely ignored the lot of them and sipped confidently on her alcohol–free cocktail.

"What's the update with Andy?" she asked.

"Everything's good. Really good. We're going to submit the divorce papers as soon as he goes back. No point in delaying it anymore… may as well get it done and out of the way. The only thing is, we need our tax returns done for last year before we can apply. But other than that, the process *seems* fairly straightforward. Prince Edward Island isn't Slovakia, after all."

"Very funny."

"Anyway, I can't imagine the courts there are too busy with divorces. There's like a hundred and fifty thousand people on the island, tops."

"How's Andy taking it?"

"A little too well," I smiled. "He never wanted to get married anyway, so I guess the divorce is just another formality. My concern is more about how much I'll have to chase him to get the papers submitted. It's almost impossible to get him to do something straight away. At this stage, I'm just keen to get it over and done with. I wouldn't feel right about dating again without it being done, or at least in progress."

"Dating, huh? Do you have anyone in particular in mind?" she enquired archly.

I grinned back at her. "All I'll say is, it's nice to feel like I'm ready to move on."

"If you say so," Michaela replied, one eyebrow raised over her cocktail.

"I feel like I've been in a long sleep, romantically. I haven't had to think about what I want for a *very* long time. Personality, looks, what's important to me, bla bla bla, etcetera etcetera. Up until my late twenties it was mostly casual flirtations. Then there was Józef… he was never in love with me. What a mess that was! Then there was Andy… definitely not a romantic, either. But we always got along very well. And he never messed me around. Now I have the extra complication of the kids. Not that I'm complaining. But realistically, I know guys will assume I'm looking for a father figure for them, and I'm not."

"They already have a father."

"Exactly. But I'm scared they'll think that's what I'm looking for, and will be put off by the idea."

"If they don't bother to find that out, then they're not the one for you."

"You're very right."

"Anyway, there's more to it than that. It's about where you're at in life, and where they're at, and how you fit together within that framework."

"It's true. I used to have such absolute ideals: the guy must be older, he must be tall, he must have this unshakeable sense of authority, he must be ambitious, he must be driven, he must look like Mr Darcy from Jane Austen. But oftentimes, I've found this type of guy to be… how to put it?"

"An illusion?"

"Well, let's just say those qualities sound better on paper. Combined in one person, and they're…"

"An illusion."

I smiled. "An illusion."

"And don't forget a boring illusion."

"At the end of the day, holding out for an imaginary ideal is stupid. All I want is someone uncomplicated. Depth. Intelligence. Decency. No games, no hidden agenda. Someone who's not afraid to hold my hand. A food lover too would be nice," I mused.

"Sounds dangerously like another ideal."

"Yes, but a more realistic one, perhaps. Ah, I wish I could understand men. They never behave in the way they're supposed to."

"I hear you."

To the disappointment of the grinning drunk, we left immediately after that drink. It was already past eleven, and Michaela had an appointment first thing in the morning. As for me, I was thoroughly knackered.

It was still very lively out on the streets at that time of night. Trams collected the tipsy and deposited fresh visitors onto Námestie SNP. People were still coming and going in the cafés and restaurants along the square and throughout the historic old town.

I suddenly remembered Ján telling me about how much it had changed over the past few years. As a schoolboy, he and his friends ran the risk of getting beaten up by skinheads if they ventured downtown. Now, you were more likely to be confronted by a latte. It was hard to imagine it being any other way.

Michaela and I walked through the crowds up to Hodžovo námestie. We hugged and parted at the underpass, promising to go out at least one more night before Andy returned to Canada.

CHAPTER THIRTY-THREE

And, just like that, the anniversary of our arrival cantered up before I knew it. I couldn't believe it had been a full year since we'd stepped off the plane, into that taxi, and onwards through the fields of wind turbines towards Bratislava.

I felt like a completely different person. I *was* a completely different person. For sure, not everything had gone to plan along the way, and there had been times when I genuinely wanted to pack it all in and scream defeat. But I didn't, and I was extraordinarily proud of myself for my resilience, and for doing it alone. If nothing else, I hoped that I'd set an example for my children as they tackled their own lives.

I was incredibly grateful to the people who'd supported me along the way: the close friends as well as the unintentional bit players. People like Michaela and Ján meant a lot to me, for very different reasons.

As for Andy, we were in a very good place. We'd managed well the transition from husband and wife to friends and co–parents. I couldn't imagine how often two divorcing parties got along so well, particularly with the upbringing of children as a constant source of negotiation and compromise. I was tremendously lucky in that Andy was generally willing to cede decision–making to me, and was supportive of all my plans. I couldn't ask for a better ex–husband. I figured it would only be a matter of time before he met someone else. He swore he would never get married again, and declared himself reluctant to live with another woman. Time would tell if he'd change his mind on either front.

And Józef? It had been more than two months since I'd last heard from him. As sudden as his reappearance in my life had been, as abrupt had been his retreat. I would always be fond of him for the sake of the past, but I had at long last learned to tell the difference between reality and nostalgia. Perhaps I was wrong in my interpretation, but love for him seemed a completely separate and non–essential component of a long–term relationship. In this respect, we were – and always had been – utterly incompatible. But he had never tried to fool me: his terms had always been there for me to see if I'd just opened my eyes. Yet a small voice within me whispered that I had, despite our differences, been a challenge to his beliefs; perhaps at times a nearly irresistible one. But, enough of all this wondering. I'd always be grateful to him for leading me to where I was now; my heart forever indebted for the extraordinary freedom that he had indirectly delivered by coming back into my life with that *hiya*. With his unwitting mission accomplished, it was time for me to move on.

All in all, I loved Bratislava, and was determined to stay if I could. The city had a vibrancy to it that I'd not experienced elsewhere; a strong sense of its history combined with a passionate determination to free itself of any remaining shackles of the past and forge a new identity. I felt an affinity in that. The boys and I had come at just the right time to witness this extraordinary transformation. Although I could have done without some of the experiences I'd gone through in that first year, I had learned to be grateful for how these had made me a stronger person.

I had a very distinct feeling that even more extraordinary things would soon be coming my way. My heart and head had their own ideas about what these might include. But I had learned not to pin my hopes to any one thing or circumstance or person.

Whatever happened in the next chapter of my Bratislava story, I couldn't help but heartily agree with a John Greenleaf Whittier quote that had always inspired me:

For all sad words of tongue and pen,
The saddest are these, 'It might have been'.

Printed in Great Britain
by Amazon